WHY WEREN'T WE TOLD?

Born in Hobart in 1938, Henry Reynolds was educated at the Hobart High School and the University of Tasmania. He worked for thirty years in Townsville at James Cook University. He is currently an Australian Research Council Senior Fellow at the University of Tasmania in Launceston.

His primary research interest has been the history of Aboriginal–white relations in Australia. His publications include *Aborigines and Settlers*, *Frontier*, *The Other Side of the Frontier*, *The Law of the Land*, *Disposession*, *With the White People*, *Fate of a Free People* and *An Indelible Stain?*.

Henry Reynolds is married to Margaret Reynolds, who was for many years a senator for Queensland. They have three children.

'A powerful and often poignant account of a life's journey . . . compelling in the clarity of the issues it raises and at times profoundly moving in the recollection of people or events which have deeply affected [the author].'

Christopher Bantick, *Sunday Tasmanian*

'Reynolds has a talent for clarifying the complex and *Why Weren't We Told?* provides an accessible, personal account of key issues in the indigenous protest including Mabo, Wik, and the notion of *nullius*.'

Lindl Lawton, *The Big Issue*

'The blend of documentary evidence and personal experience provides a powerful basis for his arguments and makes compelling reading . . . Reynolds' style of writing is very accessible . . . At a time when the possibilities for reconciliation between Indigenous and non-Indigenous Australians seem limited, *Why Weren't We Told?* is timely. It is an important book for those who want to understand why they did not know. Although it does not actually provide answers, it raises many more questions about Australian identity and maturity.'

Jackie Delpero, *Overland*

'Henry Reynolds' personal account of how he became aware of the history of Indigenous Australia made a strong impact on the judges, who agreed that his book is a timely exploration of how an individual has come to terms with an unsettling past. In addition to praising the book for its literary merit, the judges admired the author's skill in communicating his own uncomfortable feelings as an awareness of past and present injustices occurred. They felt that many Australians would relate to Henry Reynolds' early experiences of not knowing enough about the past. His book will contribute greatly to the Reconciliation debate by inspiring readers to actively seek out knowledge and understanding about Indigenous history.'

1999 Human Rights Medals and Awards Committee

Also by Henry Reynolds

WHY WEREN'T WE TOLD?

A personal search for the
truth about our history

HENRY REYNOLDS

PENGUIN BOOKS

PENGUIN BOOKS

UK | USA | Canada | Ireland | Australia
India | New Zealand | South Africa | China

Penguin Books is part of the Penguin Random House group of companies
whose addresses can be found at global.penguinrandomhouse.com.

Penguin
Random House
Australia

First published by Penguin Books Australia Ltd, 1999
This edition published by Penguin Group (Australia), 2000

Copyright © Henry Reynolds, 1999

Typeset in Perpetua by Midland Typesetters, Maryborough, Victoria
Text designed by Melissa Fraser, Penguin Design Studio
Printed and bound in Australia by Griffin Press an Accredited ISO AS/NZS 14001
Environment Management Systems Printer

National Library of Australia
Cataloguing-in-Publication data
Reynolds, Henry, 1939– .
Why weren't we told?: A personal search for the truth about our history.
Includes index.
ISBN 978 0 14 027842 2.
1. Aborigines, Australian – Treatment – History.
2. Aborigines, Australian – Public opinion – History.
3. Aborigines, Australian – Social conditions – History.
4. Australia – Race relations. I. Title.
305.89915

penguin.com.au

MIX
Paper from
responsible sources
FSC
www.fsc.org   FSC® C009448

For Margaret

Contents

Preface to This Edition

Writing is a solitary occupation. Even when a manuscript is completed it is only read by a handful of people. And then much later a book appears and goes on sale in bookshops all over the country. With luck and reasonable publicity copies are bought, presumably often read, even discussed or argued over. But the author doesn't usually meet this widely scattered, disparate audience, know its thoughts or hear its judgements. Reviews are anxiously awaited and read with trepidation. Favourable ones can exhilarate, bad ones depress and debilitate. But there is no way of knowing whether reviewers' opinions reflect those of the reading public and whether the judgements made are generally held.

I have experienced a much greater response to *Why Weren't We Told?*, since it was first published in June 1999, than I have known following the publication of any of my earlier books. People have come up to me in the street, in restaurants and theatres wanting to talk about the book. Some of the readers I have met in this way said they had been unable to put the book down and had read it in one sitting; several declared they had sat up all night and read it cover to cover before they could go to bed. Such meetings with appreciative readers mean a lot to an author.

Quite a number of those who approached me said they had either lent their copy to friends or had bought new copies to give to family members for Christmas. When presented with books to sign I have frequently been asked to address my inscription to a child, a spouse or a friend.

It was clear to me that readers had responded to both the style and the substance. Many explained that they thought that *Why Weren't We Told?* was 'a good read'. They appreciated the personal voice, the numerous anecdotes, the unfolding of my own awareness of the nation's hidden history. I was reassured when readers said they appreciated the clear prose and ease of explanation, adding that for the first time they had really understood such contentious matters as native title, the Mabo and Wik judgements, and the controversy over the so-called black-armband view of history.

Letters arrived from all over the country. One theme that came through in them again and again was that the title *Why Weren't We Told?* summed up exactly what my correspondents themselves were feeling. They confirmed what I had earlier discovered when talking to audiences in many towns and cities. There was abroad in the Australian community a strong sense of betrayal, a belief that the version of history taught in schools and communities had been seriously lacking and had hidden many aspects of the relations between the European settlers and the indigenous people. A number of my correspondents related incidents in their own life which have now assumed greater significance than they had previously, referring to bashings witnessed and racial abuse overheard. People who had travelled to north Australia in the 1950s and 1960s concurred with my description of life there and provided me with reflections and memories of their own.

Linking many comments – both oral and written – was the sense that *Why Weren't We Told?* was a timely book, one which addressed current national issues and concerns. Reconciliation remains a major national aspiration, a collective hope for a better communal future, a crusade that many hope will overcome a dark and disturbing history. The end of the century and the millennium, and the centenary of Federation, give urgency to the cause. Many Australians believe that now is the moment for a decisive change of direction, that now is the time to transcend the surviving legacy of colonialism.

At the heart of this movement is the desire to face up to our history, to embrace the past in all its aspects, to cease trying to hide the violence, the dispossession, the deprivation. People now want to know the truth about the past and to come to terms with it. They see this as an essential step along the way towards national maturity.

I would like to think that this new edition of *Why Weren't We Told?* might in some small way assist that process.

Acknowledgements

I would like to thank those people who have been directly involved in the evolution of this book. Robert Sessions and Laurie Critchley first suggested the project to me and Robert Sessions was willing to provide the support necessary to bring it to fruition. Jean Willoughby converted my often jumbled hand-written chapters into a professional manuscript.

My greatest debt is to all those people – migloo and murri alike – far too numerous to note individually, who have, over thirty years, in innumerable ways helped me to know of, think about and try to come to terms with white Australia's black history.

Terminology

There is no generally accepted terminology pertaining to the history of relations between Aborigines and Torres Strait Islanders on the one hand and settlers on the other.

Race is a discredited concept, and yet the term race relations is still convenient, as are the related terms black and white.

The term settler carries with it connotations of peaceful, uncontested annexation.

British refers to immigrants from the British Isles, but does not account for newcomers from continental Europe, Asia or the Pacific Islands.

I have used the terms whitefella and blackfella because they have such wide currency within Aboriginal society. I have also had recourse to two Queensland Aboriginal terms – murri for an Aborigine and migloo for a European.

To be consistent, I have decided to use all these terms without special emphasis, underlining, italics or inverted commas.

I

Introduction

Why were we never told? Why didn't we know? I have been asked these questions by many people, over many years, in all parts of Australia – after political meetings, after public forums, lectures, book readings, interviews. It hasn't mattered where I spoke, what size the audience, what the occasion or the actual topic dealt with.

Why didn't we know? Why were we never told?

Why do the same questions recur so frequently as though many people, at different times and in different places, were reading from one script?

Why do so many people ask the same questions of themselves, of me, of their education, their heritage, of the whole of Australian society?

In the rushed, much-interrupted conversations which take place at the end of lectures or forums, neither questions nor answers can be detailed or deeply considered. But I think what my many interrogators suggest is that they found the things I said personally significant to them. More to the point, they felt that they should have known these things themselves, and didn't. They wished they had known them before. They believed their education should have provided the knowledge, the information, and hadn't done so. They felt let down, cheated, sold short.

Why were they never told? Why didn't they know?

In answering these questions it seemed necessary to turn the question around. How was it that I had the knowledge, the information, the necessary insights? How had I come by them? The fact that I was an academic, a professional historian, that I was paid to write, research and question, would be an easy but inadequate answer. Why had I chosen to spend so many years researching the relations between indigenous and immigrant Australians? What was the cause of my obsession? My education had been quite conventional – no doubt similar to that of many in my audiences. I had a standard state-school education in Tasmania – primary school from 1944 to 1949, secondary school during 1950 to 1954. I suspect it might have been slightly better than average, but not by all that much. I was certainly not taught about any of those things which now seem so important – matters relating to race, ethnicity, indigenous Australia, land rights, self-determination, multiculturalism. There were great gaps in what I was taught. It seems from today's perspective that I learnt very little about Australia itself, certainly not enough to prepare me to be an adequate citizen, a well-informed voter and a participant in public life.

The extent of that deficiency was not apparent to me at the time. My education seemed appropriate; appeared adequate. Obviously some teachers were much better, more inspiring, than others. Some subjects provided me with skills or knowledge or insight that has gone on being useful or relevant to life.

My teachers, for their part, never suggested that they were not satisfied with the subjects they were required to teach.

By the time I had completed my undergraduate and honours degrees I had discovered disciplines that I wished I knew more about – philosophy and economics, for instance – but that had been a matter of choice on my part.

A two-year sojourn in Europe made me realise that there were many aspects of cultural life that I knew very little about – painting and sculpture, architecture, music, opera, ballet, for instance. In all of these areas I found I was ill-informed and I set about teaching myself as much as I could in a short time using the vast public resources in the galleries, museums, concert halls and opera houses of London and half a dozen other European towns and cities.

But I felt ignorant and ill-informed in a different way when I returned to Australia to take up a job at the Townsville University College at the end of 1965. I was suddenly confronted with aspects of Australian life that I knew nothing about, things I had not even suspected. It was as though I had come to a country that was both familiar and foreign at one and the same time.

I met Aborigines and Torres Strait Islanders. I saw their poverty and the way they were often treated. I heard white Australians talk about them and to them. I began to understand the complex web of social relations, habits, customs and beliefs which both bound white and black together and yet held them far apart. There was a history at work, a powerful all-important history which pressed heavily on the present. I knew nothing about it even though I had both honours and a masters degree in history.

There had been nothing in my education on which to draw, to understand many of the things I was witness to, or things that I heard about from others. I knew little about the history of Aboriginal–European relations, nothing about contact and conflict on the frontier. I had no idea there had been massacres and punitive expeditions. I was ignorant about protective and repressive legislation and of the ideology and practice of white racism beyond a highly generalised view that 'we' had treated 'them' rather badly in the past. It was a view that at least had the right orientation but it was ill-informed, sentimental and of little depth.

I can't even remember having discussed such questions with anyone in all the hundreds of hours of student discourse and disputation. I had some awareness of the agitation to repeal the White Australia Policy. I was in favour of reform and had actually argued that way in a university debating competition. But I don't think it was a matter that concerned me all that much.

So in answering the oft-asked questions: Why were we never told? Why didn't we know? I explain that I too didn't know, that I wasn't told, but came to an understanding of race relations in Australia as a result of living in North Queensland and spending years of research in libraries and archives all around Australia and overseas.

This book, then, is written for those Australians who feel they were never told and wish they had been, for those who don't realise they were never told and may not want to know anyway, and for those, mainly younger, Australians who have been told much more but who can't understand the attitudes of those who weren't given their opportunities.

As well as explaining how I have arrived at certain conclusions and adopted particular points of view, I will discuss what I currently think about a range of questions of national significance. It is a book of opinions. Many may also find it opinionated. In my own defence I can say that my views are based on things I have seen and heard, as much as they are on reading and research, and that many of them have changed and evolved over long periods of time. They have not come easily or quickly.

Some of these opinions are about Australian history – about frontier violence and Aboriginal resistance, about pioneering and the Aboriginal contribution to Australian development. Some are about important contemporary political and legal questions like the Mabo and Wik cases, self-determination and sovereignty. Others relate to what can be broadly called cultural politics – issues such as white racism, guilt and shame, national identity and belonging, political correctness and the black-armband version of history.

I should begin my story with an incident, still vividly remembered, which occurred in the late 1960s soon after my arrival in North Queensland. It took place on Palm Island, a large Aboriginal settlement about 40 kilometres offshore from Townsville.

II

An Unforgettable Incident

The prison was a small concrete building, bare and featureless. It stood on its own, surrounded by open ground. It could have been a fort or a blockhouse.

'Can we see inside?' my companion Senator Jim Keefe asked the Superintendent who was conducting us on a tour of Palm Island. Without speaking he unlocked the door and we followed him into a dark vestibule. Like the outside it was bare, rough concrete. Coming in from the harsh summer sunlight we found it dark and cool. It smelt of urine. There were two doors, one in front of us, one on the right-hand side.

'There is no-one in that cell,' the Superintendent said, nodding towards the door in front of us. He turned to his right, unlocked the second door and threw it open. The walls were bare, with light coming in from a barred window. The glass on the inside of the bars had been broken and shards of it were scattered on the floor. There was a plastic bucket in the far right-hand corner. Along the wall facing the window was an old, dirty mattress flat on the concrete floor.

Sitting on the mattress were two small girls. One may have been about thirteen, the other smaller and perhaps younger. They were dressed in ill-fitting print dresses several sizes too large for them.

The Superintendent told them to stand up. They looked aghast at being seen in such a situation by visiting migloos, or whitefellas. The bigger of the two girls had one hand and lower arm bandaged. Blood had seeped through and spread on the surface of the bandage. The Superintendent explained that she had a short time before smashed the window with her fist.

'Why are they here?' Jim asked incredulously. The Superintendent explained that they had sworn at their teacher. They were spending the day in prison as a consequence. The situation and the answer were both so unexpected that we stood for a few moments in stunned silence before following the Superintendent out of the cell and back into the intense sunlight.

It happened just over thirty years ago. We were only in the prison for a few minutes but I still have a vivid memory of the incident although it was not the only disturbing or shocking thing I saw or heard on that first visit to Palm Island. But there was something about the imprisoned children which impressed itself deeply on my mind.

It was, to begin with, so unexpected. There was such a disparity between the offence and the punishment, between the locks, reinforced door, bars and thick concrete walls and the little thin girls. It was so grossly disproportionate. Having just recently taught children of a similar age in both Tasmania and England I found the punishment deeply shocking. What misuse of arbitrary power! What could the teacher have been thinking of? Did the teacher or the Superintendent or the other members of the white staff wonder what the long-term consequences of their actions would be? The Superintendent had looked a little uneasy when he was asked to open the jail – but only a little. His response suggested that the incarceration of children for minor offences was not unusual. He didn't suggest the two girls were especially difficult or hardened or were repeat offenders. Their punishment was apparently within the parameters of what was thought normal on the island.

To me it seemed so utterly out of place in the modern Australia I knew about. It wasn't the nineteenth century. It wasn't the Queensland of the wild and violent frontier. It was the year after the referendum which had been seen as a massive community endorsement of equality and the removal of discrimination.

The incident shook my belief that Australia was a society that valued equality above all other virtues and was committed to a fair go for all. It didn't fit easily into any of my assumptions about my own society. If such manifest injustice could flourish in 1968, whatever had been done in the past? If this could be done to children, whatever punishments were meted out to adults?

Why didn't I know? Why hadn't I been told?

In retrospect I realise that my reaction to things seen and heard in the north had been repeated many times over in the past, when Australians from the cities had come face to face with the continuing legacy of colonialism and either came to accept that what they saw was just the way things were done 'up north', or on the other hand refused to conform and railed against the frontier and all its works. My upbringing and education in Tasmania ensured that I would adopt the second course of action.

III

The Innocence of an Island Education

Growing up in Hobart I had little awareness of Aborigines, or of race, or of north Australia for that matter. I occasionally heard that there were people called half-castes who lived on the Bass Strait islands. But they were remote places – no more than marks on the map. I don't think I knew anyone who had actually been there. As far as I can recall, the first time I saw an Aborigine was when we were on our way to England in 1964. The ship berthed in Brisbane and we went into town for the day. In a crowded street I saw a young Aboriginal man. I thought it a memorable experience.

I had met a Torres Strait Islander in unusual circumstances when I was about fourteen. He had come to Hobart as a crew member of a ship delivered to new owners. He had a few days to spare before he returned to Queensland but found Hobart very unfriendly. My older sister saw him at a dance. She was the only person who would dance with him. A few days later she brought him home for a meal, to the considerable surprise of my parents.

11

After he had gone my father said that Islanders were of a higher and more advanced race than the Aborigines. Several days later the Islander rang and asked me to go to the pictures with him as he didn't want to go on his own. I was far less courageous than my sister and found the prospect far too embarrassing, so I rebuffed all his entreaties and said I had too much homework to do.

But we grew up in Tasmania with a sense of an Aboriginal past. There were middens at the back of many of the beaches where we picnicked and everyone knew what they were. People I knew collected stone tools, or flints as we called them. As a child I was fascinated by a diorama in the museum which depicted an Aboriginal couple seated by a camp fire where a crayfish was cooking. Looking on and standing by their side was a boy of six or seven. We were regular museum visitors so I stood in front of the diorama many times. I can still recall much of the detail. I was most interested in the little boy and wondered about him and what sort of games he would play.

My father often told me stories about places we visited or passed on the road – the scene of a battle between Aborigines and redcoats, the site of Governor Arthur's camps as he conducted the Black Line across the island in 1830. He told me how his aunt, who had brought him up, talked of Truganini, who was one of the characters about town up until the time of her death in 1876.

Tasmanians had the sense that the Aborigines were important in the early history of the colony. The story of the Black War, the Black Line, the Friendly Mission, were among the things which made island history distinctive. The Aborigines were never written out of local history. It was widely believed that the Tasmanians were a unique race unrelated to mainland Aborigines.

The death of Truganini in 1876 was treated as an event of great significance – the occasion either for sentimental regret or for denunciation as the final event in one of history's few case studies of genocide.

But, whichever view was favoured, there was widespread agreement in both popular and specialist literature that the Tasmanians had been a uniquely primitive people. They were living fossils, representatives of the 'old Stone Age'. As such, it was inevitable that they would be propelled rapidly towards extinction by the iron laws of evolution, which were outside human control.

This was certainly the message embodied in an extract, reprinted in my Grade 6 reading book, entitled 'Extinct Hunters: The Tasmanians' by a Dr W.J. Solas. The race, we were informed, became extinct with the death of Truganini. But the message of the extract was that the Tasmanians were interesting because they had been so primitive; they were important because they had died out. The implication for mainland Aborigines was clear. They too would tread the downward path already walked by the Tasmanians. The progress could be delayed by humane treatment but the fate of the race was sealed. This was certainly the view that I can remember adults espousing when I overheard snatches of their conversation. Any discussion about the Aboriginal 'question' seemed to end with the remark that 'anyway they are dying out'. There seemed to be no comeback once the collective death sentence had been passed. It both cut short debate and obviated the need for thought about the future.

During four years of secondary education, history, geography and economics were combined in a social studies syllabus that was accompanied by a set of textbooks called *Out of the Mist,* which attempted to provide an overview of world history. The under-lying theme was social evolution. It told the story of 'Man's Emergence from the Mists of Savagery' and his slow upward struggle towards civilisation. Consequently the Aborigines were studied at the very beginning of the first year. They were Stone Age people who belonged at the dawn of time; they had scarcely emerged from the mist. As for the Tasmanians, they were uniquely primitive:

> When the white settlers came to Tasmania they found one of
> the most primitive races in the world, and, as often happens
> when the civilised meet the primitive, annihilated them.

Having been given an invidious part at the very beginning of humanity's upward journey the Aborigines did not appear again in later years or succeeding books. The deficiency was not reme-died in my fifth and final year at high school. In fact there was nothing at all about Australia, as far as I can remember, in the history, geography or literature syllabus.

My undergraduate education at the University of Tasmania was similar. Although I studied history, politics and literature, little attention was devoted to Australia. In three years of history I studied Europe, America and Asia. There was no course in Aus-tralian history although it was possible to pursue a few local topics in a subject on the British Empire and Commonwealth which held little interest for me. In three years of English litera-ture we only considered two Australian books – one novel, Henry Handel Richardson's *The Fortunes of Richard Mahony*, and a short-story collection. We read no Australian poetry or drama. We learnt nothing about local cultural movements, nor was it ever suggested that they might be important. In political science the story was much the same. In three years we dealt with Australia during one term and then only as part of a much wider consideration of federalism, which seemed to be a serious enough topic to allow Australia to gain entry into cosmopolitan discourse.

I began to read Australian history as an honours student in 1959 and as a masters student during 1961–62. My reading was selective – Tasmania specifically and Australia generally in the late nineteenth century. I read avidly, but I didn't come across anything that would have prepared me to understand race relations in north Australia. There was little of relevance available. Even if there had been I might have been uninterested in it. When Aborigines appeared in the general literature it was invariably in the early years of settlement – around the fledgling towns of Sydney and Hobart or out on the frontier where they sometimes assisted and sometimes harassed explorers and pioneers. But such encounters were depicted as having taken place a long time ago, in the early days. The books which gave me a rudimentary grasp of national history provided no sense of ongoing problems or of recurring conflict. Past and present did not seem to be related.

When I was working on my MA thesis I was asked to teach an evening course of Australian history at the Hobart Technical College for young Commonwealth public servants seeking promotion. The set textbook was Ernest Scott's *A Short History of Australia*. It was first published in 1916 and had been reprinted many times. It was scarcely the latest word on history although it did provide a fairly comprehensive survey of exploration, settlement and political development. Scott explained how the story

15

of Australia began with a 'blank space on the map' which was progressively filled in as a result of European endeavour. Aborigines were not given much of a run. They were mentioned four times in all — three times just in passing. There was also a brief discussion which ran to about two pages out of a book of 376 pages. The first references were to the attitudes of the early explorers. Dampier, Scott noted, thought the Aborigines utterly repellent — they were black, ugly, flyblown, blinking creatures and the most unpleasant human beings he had ever encountered. Dampier observed that the Aborigines were pestered by flies. But it was Scott's idea that they were flyblown. In the only passage of any substance Scott dealt with frontier conflict. It was perfunctory but it did not disguise the brutality involved. The tragedy of the process was, he wrote, very grim and hateful. Scott assumed that the indigenous story was almost completed, the end both known and in sight. The Aborigines were not a people who could be absorbed or who could adapt to civilised life, and in the more populated parts of the country they were 'fading out of existence very rapidly, and within the present generation will probably cease to exist'.

Although we used the book for months, referring to it constantly, none of the students found the treatment of the Aborigines insufficient, dismissive or racist. Nor did I.

In the Tasmania of my childhood one learnt little about racial or cultural diversity. It was a remarkably homogeneous society even in terms of island history. It was more homogeneous in the 1940s than it had been in the colonial era and more so than it was to become in the postwar period. Almost everyone was of Anglo-Saxon-Celtic origin and, given the low level of in-migration, most people had been born in Tasmania. Apart from a few

16

Chinese-Tasmanian families who ran fruit and vegetable stores, I don't remember meeting any non-European people at all during my childhood. As far as I can recall I did not see any African-Americans among the thousands of American service-men whose ships berthed in Hobart before sailing north into the war zone. I have no recollection of anyone in my primary school who by name or physical characteristics was other than of main-stream British stock. Even among them, the differences of region and dialect their ancestors had brought from Europe had been ironed out in Tasmania. I remember an incident which illus-trates this. It was the day that the first postwar migrant children arrived at school.

I knew something was going on as soon as I walked in the gate. As I looked down onto the playground from the terrace I could see that large numbers of children were clustered around someone or something. It obviously wasn't a fight because there was little movement and no noise. As I walked down the stairs I saw that everyone was gathering around three new kids – a big boy and younger twin sisters. They were remarkable because they were so different. Their clothes were unusual and they spoke in a way we could scarcely understand. I joined the crowd as we followed them across the yard. We couldn't take our eyes off them. We heard later from the teachers that the strangers were from Liverpool and that we had to welcome them. That wasn't a view that was universally shared. The tough boys of the school kept trying to pick a fight with the boy, but he seemed quite able to defend himself.

Within a year or so another group of foreigners made their appearance in our neighbourhood. They had come to lay a water pipeline through our streets. The work gang was made up of refugees from many countries in Eastern and Central Europe. My friends and I were fascinated by them and during the summer holidays would go and talk with them when they had either lunch or smoko. My sister and I were so interested in the 'Balts' and 'reffos' who appeared in increasing numbers that we would pretend to talk to one another in loud voices in a language of our own making, and were delighted when people stared at us. We were young enough to be excited rather than threatened by the sudden appearance of foreigners. We were exhilarated by difference.

While young Tasmanians knew little about race and ethnicity, they were thoroughly schooled in class distinction. Hobart was – and still is – remarkably class-segregated given its relatively small size. My family didn't fit easily into the well-established patterns of class and location. We lived in a stately Federation house on a large block which included an orchard, with sweeping views of the Derwent. But it was in the wrong part of town, in a predominantly working- and lower-middle-class suburb. That may have added to the great emphasis that was always put on correct speech, polite manners, discreet behaviour and all those other points of etiquette which showed we weren't 'common'.

My older brother and sister attended a small private college at the far end of the suburb, which closed the year before I went to school. After much agonising, my parents decided to send me to the local state school or to the one that seemed less belligerently working-class. In the schoolyard I entered another world – one where a militant egalitarianism ruled. It derived partly from mainstream Australian working-class culture of the period. But I suspect that there was an additional militancy in the rejection of pretence and snobbery derived from Hobart's convict/emancipist heritage, which lived on with undiminished vigour.

How intensely we derided any suggestion of affectation or the slightest assumption of superiority. I vividly remember the way we hated a young solicitor who lived with his mother in the cul-de-sac we used as our meeting place, cricket pitch and football ground. His offence in our eyes was that he wore his wavy hair a little longer than normal and swept back, rather than having it parted on one side. Even more provocative in our eyes was that when he drove his car he wore leather gloves and occasionally even sported a cravat. We shouted abuse and sometimes threw stones as he motored disdainfully past.

My easy and complete conversion to schoolyard egalitarianism owed something to my family circumstances. For several of my most formative years my two grandmothers lived with us. Until I was seven I was the youngest member of the extended family of grandmothers, parents and two older siblings. At a very early age I became aware of my situation at the bottom of the hierarchy. I can remember telling myself many times over that everyone could tell me what to do whereas I had no-one to exercise authority over. What made it especially galling was that it often happened that several people would give me different and conflicting instructions. It was even more infuriating when the adults closed ranks and wouldn't admit that they were the cause of the confusion. My brother lacked legitimate authority but used cruder methods of coercion and persuasion, which were hard to resist even if doing so earned rebukes from the grown-ups. These were early lessons in injustice, and fostered an anti-authoritarian streak which helped shape habits and reactions of a lifetime.

In my fourth year at university I was able to choose a topic for a history honours thesis. It was the first serious piece of historical work I had done. With little hesitation I decided on Australian history and focused on the radical nationalist literature of the 1890s. Many of the writers were new to me or had only been names before. Their larrikin egalitarianism was both familiar and exciting. I not only analysed their ideas, I glorified them. This, I felt, was the essence of Australia.

I appreciated, too, the celebration of mateship. That too I instinctively understood. It sanctified and gave nationalist legitimacy to the loud, larrikin camaraderie of the university football team and the close, warm companionship of drunken hours in the front bar with the boys.

There was much about the radical nationalist traditions that I either didn't notice at the time or wasn't sensitive to. It is obvious now that it was extremely blokey, often to the point of misogyny. There didn't seem to be anything unusual about that. New-wave feminism was still a decade away. The party was not yet over. With deeper reflection I might have sensed that egalitarianism, in a culturally homogeneous society like the Tasmania I had grown up in, very easily lurches into narrow-minded conformity and hostility to even minor differences of speech, dress, gesture, demeanour. That was why we hurled rocks at the young solicitor who had the temerity to wear leather gloves while at the wheel of his car.

But given what my future held, it was the intense racism of the 1890s that I most significantly and conspicuously failed to notice. And it was so obvious in many of the texts I read that year. The equality so exalted was the equality of white men of British descent. Non-Europeans – Asians, Pacific Islanders, Aborigines – had no place in the radical utopia. They couldn't aspire to equality and had to be excluded. They could be vilified, denigrated and abused. Non-Europeans threatened to corrupt society, under-mine democracy and pollute the pure blood of the white master race. The fact that these ideas had real, dramatic and damaging impact on Aborigines, Chinese and Pacific Islanders in Australia at the turn of the century was lost on me. The fact that the heroic bushmen had bloodstained hands was a discovery that awaited me some distance down my own intellectual track.

While I was tardy in recognising the racism embedded in the heart of radical nationalism, I was fortunate in growing up at the precise moment when, suddenly and dramatically, race lost its discursive power. The war against fascism, the shocking revela-tions of the Holocaust, discredited the whole legacy of social Darwinism, eugenics and race science. The biology, anthropol-ogy and historiography which surrounded and supported the concept of race were instantly and profoundly discredited. At much the same time European power shrank dramatically. As I passed through primary school the old empires crumbled. The prewar maps on our classroom walls no longer reflected the state of the world. They rapidly became charts of vanished hegemony. Decolonisation gathered momentum and was unstoppable. Even when quite young I thought it was an exciting and wholly positive development, with new nations, new flags and exotic new postage stamps.

After 1945, Australian egalitarianism was able to move in the world without the burden of white racism. It could stretch out beyond the boundaries erected by race and blood and ethnicity. My contemporaries could and in my experience did welcome con-tinental European migrants into our secondary school and Asian students into our universities. We wanted to be cosmopolitan. We supported multiculturalism before the term itself was coined.

A two-year stay in Europe challenged some ideas while strengthening others. My new-world chauvinism was undermined by the old world's depth of history and richness of culture. London offered intellectual and cultural stimulation scarcely imaginable in Hobart. Much of Australia's swagger and irreverence seemed to be a reaction to the fate of isolation and provincialism. But that did not suggest to me a return to the pro-British devotion of many older Tasmanians, who still talked about 'going home' and did so when we announced our plans to take the big white boat back along the sea lanes of Empire. That was no answer. It promised to condemn us to perpetual provincialism – to endlessly adopt last year's fashions, discarded designs, tired ideas; always to live a derivative, second-hand life and always to be patronised by the metropolitans and to be resentful in return.

As much as I was delighted by English landscape and English light I never felt really at home. It wasn't my country, however rich the literary associations. The nineteenth-century migration of forebears had done its work. There was no longer any way back to Europe other than to live as a visitor, a sojourner, an outsider.

There was also no place in the English class structure where we felt comfortable. And how deep, powerful and obvious class differences were. In that way England conformed to our Australian prejudices. The weight of class oppression was very obvious when teaching in a secondary school in the East End and living in a still-poor working-class Islington. But the imprint of class was everywhere: in the poor, pinched lives of many in the East End and their fatalistic acceptance of poverty and the improbability of upward social mobility; in the chilly punctiliousness and wary snobbery of those in the middle; and in the breathtaking arrogance and self-assurance of the upper classes.

But the London of the 1960s was also grappling with questions of race, as immigrants from both the West Indies and south Asia became very visible minorities. For the first time we had black colleagues, friends, landlords, neighbours. Racial tension and controversy were impossible to avoid. Elderly English people confided in us that they really welcomed us despite the tightening of immigration laws. We were white and were kin. A young black woman abused me on a bus when I moved away from her to sit next to Margaret when a seat became available, assuming it to be a racist insult. Landlords advertised flats with cards which contained the words 'no coloureds'. West Indian children were just beginning to turn up at my school in Hackney. As the numbers increased, the Cockney kids complained that their neighbourhoods were being invaded and taken over. When a new child was bashed on the way to school, the headmaster – a small, mild man – caned the perpetrators with passion and conviction although such violence was clearly against his nature. Arguments about racism broke out in buses, with many passengers joining in. There was overt racism about, but there was also spirited resistance to it.

At Hyde Park Corner race and colonialism were more commonly discussed than older concerns about class or religion. One morning we joined a crowd listening to an articulate and fiery young African man. To our embarrassment he was being heckled by a party of young Australians. Among other things they told him was that there was no racial prejudice in Australia because everyone there was equal. With that the speaker turned on the hecklers and launched a tirade about Australia's treatment of the Aborigines. He was probably better informed about the matter than were the Australians in his audience, myself included. He scorned the hecklers for being ignorant about their own history.

For the first time I heard mention of the Queensland Native Police. It was a premonition, as we were preparing to leave Europe, of what was to face us in our new life in north Australia.

It was only by chance that we went there. We certainly had no intention of going there when we set off for Europe. We thought we would go back to Tasmania or to nearby areas of mainland Australia. The job offer from the Townsville University College came out of the blue. I had seen an advertisement for it in the English papers but had not been interested in it even though we were looking for ways to get back to Australia. I had applied, unsuccessfully, for a lectureship at the University of Queensland, but the job went to someone else. When, at short notice, the person appointed to the Townsville job changed his mind about moving north they looked again at my application.

Quite unexpectedly I was asked by telegram to go into central London for an interview. A few days later a second telegram arrived, offering me a job with fares paid back to Australia. On a train journey through the grey half-light of the English country-side deep in winter we discussed whether I should accept the offer. While we wanted to return – and needed to do so or face the prospect of paying two years of English taxation – we knew nothing about Townsville. We didn't know exactly where it was and didn't have a map of Australia with us to place it correctly in that sequence of provincial cities which notch Queensland's long coastline. We didn't know it was so far north of Brisbane, so deep in the tropics.

We assumed that Aborigines would be living in or near Townsville and in our discussions about our new life we agreed that we should 'do something for them'. What or how or whether such help would be welcome were questions that didn't occur to us. I had been struck by the response of my teaching colleagues in Burnie, when, soon after I arrived in 1960, a popular couple on the staff resigned to go north and work on an Aboriginal mission. It was seen as both an adventurous and idealistic thing to do. So in July 1965 Margaret, eight-month-old John and I sailed from Genoa. After a fortnight in Tasmania I flew north, feeling very much a pioneer, while Margaret and John stayed on in Launceston until I had 'settled in'.

IV

Travelling North

In 1965 it took two and a half hours to fly from Brisbane to Townsville. As the plane droned on and on I realised how far I was flying away from my own country. The land below was harsh and unfamiliar. And it was so vast, so empty. The small towns were each so isolated from one another and so overwhelmed by the land itself. When the plane eventually landed, the brief tropical twilight was over. The night was dark and warm and close even at that time of year. When I saw the small wooden hut which served in those days as the terminal, and the bright yellow fluorescent lights swarming with insects, I had serious doubts about our decision to come north.

Townsville itself was not what I had expected. It was certainly different, but it was neither exotic nor picturesque. There was none of the green tropical lushness I was expecting. There was little greenery at all. I arrived at the end of the long dry season, which had succeeded an unusually poor wet season. Water was scarce. Gardens, parks, open space, the hills around were burnt off and bare. Clumps of dead grass collected wind-blown rubbish. Most of the houses stood up on stumps, perched uneasily between the baked earth and the vast vitreous sky. Townsville scarcely seemed to be a city at all. There was only one long main street, squeezed in between mud and mangroves on one side and the pink–brown granite of Castle Hill on the other. The sun arched high overhead. The shadows were short, sharp and intense. Many of the older people bore on their arms, necks and faces the ravages of a lifetime in the tropics.

Almost everything was different – the light, the sky, the birds, insects, trees, the sounds and smells. But there was much that immediately appealed – brief, brilliant twilights, moon-drenched nights and, above all, the trade winds. They were nothing like the chilly, rough tumult of the Roaring Forties. They were constant and even, as smooth and cool as silk.

Townsville was a very masculine society. Blokes in blue singlets walked with an easy swagger. It was a town of big bluff voices, hearty laughs, hard handshakes. If you didn't seem too different it was friendly and accommodating. It was a strong union town. Memories were still alive of the time when it was known as the Red North, and Communist Party officials were influential in the Trades and Labour Council. Women were expected to know their place. When Margaret arrived, a few weeks after I had settled in, she was invited to join an organisation called the Townsville University College Staff and Distaff Association. She went to an alfresco morning tea to which the wives wore gloves and stockings and the talk was of shopping and children.

In many respects Townsville society was similar to that found in other parts of provincial Australia, not all that different from Burnie, where I had taught in 1960–61. But what made it more than a larger, warmer Burnie was that it was deep within what, in 1971, Charles Rowley was to call colonial Australia – that part of the country with significant numbers of Aborigines and Torres Strait Islanders, where the traditions, behaviour and attitudes of the frontier era persisted and where race relations were a major cause of friction, a constant topic of discussion and debate. There had perhaps never been a time in North Queensland's hundred years of white history when the 'Aboriginal question' had not been a matter of contention among the settlers and their Australian-born descendants.

In the late 1960s Aborigines and Torres Strait Islanders were moving into Townsville in unprecedented numbers. It was part of a process of indigenous urbanisation that was at work all over Australia. Restrictions were being lifted on the movement of people resident on reserves and missions, and there was even encouragement for families to leave the once-closed communities. New policies were beginning to reverse those in place since 1897 to sweep up all Aborigines living in and around the towns and confine them to isolated settlements. Palm Island families began to settle permanently in Townsville. At much the same time pastoralists were forcing Aboriginal stockworkers off their stations once they were required to pay them award wages. The Torres Strait Islanders who, as contract labourers, had rebuilt the Townsville – Mt Isa railway line in the early 1960s stayed behind to get jobs and began to bring their families to mainland Australia, initiating a process of chain migration which continues to this day.

When we arrived in Townsville, Aborigines and Islanders were the only substantial and visible minority in a community that had received far fewer non-English-speaking migrants than the major urban centres. They made up somewhere between 5 and 10 per cent of the population and were immediately noticeable. Numerous families shared large dilapidated wooden houses, in or near the central business district, which either blew down during Cyclone Althea in 1971 or were subsequently bull-dozed to make way for office blocks or units. Because of the enormous difficulties which faced indigenous families trying to find cheap rental accommodation, many of the houses were seri-ously overcrowded. Families were large and children of all ages played in the bare yards, their games spilling out onto nearby footpaths to the obvious annoyance of passing pedestrians. Ephemeral groups of Aborigines lived out in camps around the outskirts of the town in clumps of trees or bushes or in amongst the mangroves. Fluctuating numbers of men, women and chil-dren continued to fish and forage for food, keeping vestiges of their ancient economy alive. The camps often shifted and waxed and waned as people moved to and from Palm Island or the small towns in the interior. Quite large parties walked through town and suburbs in long straggling lines as they must have done in the centuries before the coming of the Europeans. Loud laughter, shouted conversation or fierce arguments announced their pres-ence, arousing insecurity and hostility in tidy white suburbs. White fears were even more pronounced in the dark, as we dis-covered one hot night.

Our daughters, Anna and Rebecca, and I were washing up under open windows which looked out onto a vacant block. We started to sing. I think we sang 'Click Go the Shears'. We accom-panied ourselves by banging spoons on saucepans, plates and glasses. We were quite pleased with our efforts even though the performance prolonged the task. Soon after we had finished both concert and washing up, we noticed several people walking back and forth over the vacant block with flashlights in their hands. A few minutes later a neighbour rang. He lived on the other side of the block. He shouted into the phone, obviously agitated: 'Did you hear them! Did you hear them? It was the Aborigines. They were having a corroboree. I called the police but by the time they arrived the abos had gone. It's got something to do with this land rights business.'

It took me a few seconds to realise that it was our singing that had aroused his fears. I was too amazed to laugh, too surprised to own up. But he finished with a comment I had heard several times before: 'It's the women and kiddies I'm worried about. I can look after myself.' There was something sinister in his assertion. I recalled soon after that he was an ex-British commando who had guns in his house and knew how to use them.

The indigenous community, which to the whites was largely undifferentiated, was quite diverse and internally divided. The most obvious division was between Aborigines and Torres Strait Islanders. Few Europeans were aware that the Islanders came from three distinct island groups, eastern, central and western; that they had separate languages; and that the eastern and western languages were mutually unintelligible. Historically the three groups had engaged in periodic bouts of warfare. There was more mixing between the groups in Townsville than there ever had been in Torres Strait itself.

The Islanders came from their various and disparate islands, like other immigrants from rural villages in southern Europe, to get work and so escape poverty. They came with little experience of Australian society and for many years had been prevented from landing on the mainland, although many men had sailed their luggers far down the Queensland coast collecting trochus shell. Their experience of colonisation was very different from that of the Aborigines. The missionaries had arrived in Torres Strait before the government. There was little interest among Europeans in land on small, isolated and already heavily populated islands, although generations of Island men were drawn into the maritime industries of pearling, trochus and bêche-de-mer collecting. The Queensland authorities adopted a form of indirect rule in Torres Strait which gave the Islanders a significant degree of autonomy, thereby preserving their own form of government and lines of authority. So when the Islanders arrived in Townsville and other Queensland towns they came with a self-confidence which arose from having secure homelands and a culture largely preserved, albeit in modified form. Their self-assurance was apparent in their manner, their gestures, their gait. The popular and frequently expressed European view was that the Islanders were more advanced and more intelligent than the Aborigines.

The Aboriginal community was diversified as well. In Townsville there was a mixing of people from different parts of North Queensland and with varying life experiences. Some were members of families which had managed to stay on their own country by working in the pastoral industry over several generations. Others came from Palm Island. They had either been born there or had been removed from their own country and exiled offshore. Shared experience of life in Townsville, where all alike were regarded as 'Abos' and were treated accordingly, began to shape a stronger sense of Aboriginality than had ever existed before. The establishment of local branches of political organisations like the One People for Australia League (OPAL) and the Aborigines Advancement League hastened the development, as did the far greater access and exposure to the media which Townsville provided.

Though divided by culture and experience, the Aboriginal and Islander populations were united by poverty. Although quite a few men had jobs, their history of wage-earning had been brief. Whether they had worked on cattle stations or on settlements, they had little access to or experience of money, having been paid in kind or been given small sums as pocket money while the rest of their wages were paid into accounts managed by the notorious government trust fund. On both stations and settlements, rations, clothes, hats and boots were handed out on a regular basis. In such circumstances few families could accumulate savings or possessions or anything more than the basic items of clothing. Many people had arrived in Townsville with only what they stood up in. Few had any knowledge of the welfare system, benefits from which had either been denied them or subsequently paid into the central accounts of reserve or mission.

Adding to the indigenous disadvantage was the fact that, overwhelmingly, the people who moved into Townsville had little formal education – usually no more than a few years in a poorly run and underfunded settlement school. Few had any skills which received recognition in a wider society, despite work done for many years on the settlements. The complex skills of the stockman, the physical endurance of the trochus diver, had little market value in the urban setting.

So in 1966 to be black was to be poor – and often desperately poor. Many families had few clothes, few kitchen utensils or consumer goods. The children played in their yards and under the high houses boisterous or imaginative games without the benefit of toys. Because Townsville had little public transport indigenous families often spent half a day walking across the suburbs to meet friends or relatives. I had been in Townsville for several years before I saw an indigenous person driving a car. I can still remember my surprise. I told Margaret about it as soon as I got home and we wondered who the man was. Within a few years many families had become car owners.

They had begun a slow and difficult journey up from indigence. In thirty years many have succeeded. They have become home-owners and have reached a standard of living far beyond their expectations in the 1960s. It is a success story which is both individual and communal, but one which is rarely recognised by the wider community. Too often critics of indigenous policies – white and black alike – insist that nothing has changed, that large-scale government expenditure has had little impact on poverty and deprivation.

In many cases the children of those who came to town in the 1960s seized the opportunities for education denied their parents. Government and Catholic schools had their deficiencies, but they offered a far better education than that provided on the reserves and missions. The children who grew up in Townsville were favoured by a much more supportive intellectual and cultural environment than their parents had known. The American civil rights movement, decolonisation of much of the world, and the contemporaneous emergence of a powerful local indigenous political movement all provided inspiration and motivation lacking in the 1930s and 1940s. I witnessed a small but telling example of the impact of a changing world on Aboriginal children one morning on Palm Island in 1974.

I was host to the distinguished African scholar Ali Mazrui, who came to Townsville to deliver a public lecture for the local branch of the Australian Institute of International Affairs. I took him to Palm Island for the morning. We were appropriately greeted by the white manager and members of the elected, and therefore indigenous, council. The old prison had been demolished. But we did visit the new and impressive school built with federal government money. As we entered the first classroom the headmaster and manager led the way. I tagged along a few steps behind Mazrui. On the appearance of the two important migloos the children struggled out of their desks and stood to attention in the aisles. It was then that they caught sight of the important visitor. And he was a black man. Surprise and pleasure lit their faces. They stared at Mazrui, then back at one another in silent communion and then back at Mazrui. It was a magical moment. Mazrui himself was obviously touched by his reception.

The boys and girls who grew up in Townsville had not acquired their parents' ancestral fear of the migloos. They lacked that sense of subordination. They no longer 'knew their place'. By the mid-1970s one increasingly saw young black teenagers who dressed in the latest fashions with contemporary haircuts and a general sense of style to match. They felt good about themselves. They deferred to nobody. When white girls were seen out with black boys conservative townspeople were horrified. One morning I walked down Flinders Street behind a good friend of mine. He was what many people would have called a 'full-blood Aborigine'. His white wife held his arm. I was able to watch the reaction of people who caught sight of the couple approaching and then passing them. Some people scarcely noticed or showed little obvious interest. But others were shocked, confronted. They stared with obvious hostility.

Emerging black self-confidence often evoked white antago-
nism. Numerous events confirmed this phenomenon. I remember
an incident which occurred one day in the mid-1970s. I was
driving down to a neighbourhood bottle shop and passed a young
Aboriginal man of about sixteen or seventeen who was walking
along the footpath in the same direction. There was something
about him that immediately attracted my attention. It was his
walk and bearing. He gave the impression of great pride and self-
confidence. But he attracted other eyes as well as mine, as I soon
discovered.

Having passed him, I turned into the drive-in bottle shop
around a circular drive and then sat facing outward looking over
the footpath and road. The woman brought my bottle and change
and as she did so she stopped, noticing the young man walking
past. She turned to me and said angrily, 'Well, just take a look at
that nigger! He thinks he owns the place!' It was not just that we
had both noticed something special about the young man, but
that she felt completely confident that I would agree with her,
that as a white man I would be complicit with her hostility to an
'uppity blackfella'. I wasn't brave enough to say to her that I had
admired him for the very qualities she decried. I said nothing. In
remaining silent I no doubt let her assume there was solidarity
between us.

I recall another incident about this time that is equally relevant. I was at a party and got into conversation with a young
Aboriginal woman. She had grown up in Townsville, a member of
one of the large well-known local families, but had been working
in Sydney for some years. She was well dressed, stylish, articulate
and extremely self-confident. She told me how glad she was she
had gone south. People there had been so friendly and accepting.

The experience had completely changed her outlook, her attitude to migloos and to herself. She held my gaze and said, 'Do you know, before I went to Sydney, I had never once dared to look at a white person straight in the eye.'

Something else bore down on the Aborigines who settled in Townsville other than their collective poverty. Indigence alone was not sufficient to explain the situation. When I grew up in Hobart there were numerous families whose material circumstances were not much better than those experienced by indigenous people in North Queensland twenty years later. But in Tasmania the poor were feisty and aggressively egalitarian. They asserted in every way the proposition that apart from having few possessions they were as good as anyone else. They knew no deference at all. And that seemed quite natural. I'm not sure anyone thought they were 'uppity'.

What encircled Aborigines – and to a lesser extent Islanders – was an all-embracing, inherited sense of forced subordination. The young woman at the party was right. Many older Aboriginal people would not make eye contact with migloos. Culturally determined reticence or shyness was only part of the explanation for this. More compelling were the expectations of white people, which included lowered eyes and a submissive downward tilt of the head. That was the way to avoid trouble. For several years an Aboriginal woman worked for us and she became a good friend, confiding in us and seeking our help in her battles with bureaucrats and landlords. But it was many months before she was able to look directly at us when she spoke and for a long time she would not stay beside us as we walked down the street together but would hang back and remain a few steps behind. An old man told a student of mine during a taped interview that his father had constantly told him that whatever he did he must never backchat a white man, regardless of the provocation. Any hint of defiance might result in assault by fist or boot or stockwhip or all three together.

During another interview a very old lady said that she warned the young people not to get involved in politics, not to challenge the migloos in any way, because there was the ever-present danger that the children would be taken away.

The terrible past of violence and dispossession still haunted the living. It could be seen shaping social reactions, determining means of address. It could be briefly glimpsed in fleeting expressions of face or eye. Many families had their own private stories of how white men had killed, raped and brutalised their kin in their grandfather's and great-grandfather's time. They were stories of fear and terror. And with each retelling fear was recalled, and passed on, to be constantly refreshed by smaller, less significant, more recent acts of oppression – personal abuse, threats, official authoritarianism or insensitivity. Such epithets as 'boong', 'coon' and 'nigger' wounded because they had been hardened and sharpened by history. Incidents or exchanges which may have seemed insignificant to white people were often far more insulting and hurtful to indigenous people because they echoed down long corridors of subordination, humiliation and embarrassment.

Living in Townsville in daily contact with migloos was fraught with tension and anxiety for many families, as we quickly learnt from our own experience. We called on many indigenous families soon after we arrived, to see if the children would like to attend a kindergarten Margaret had established. I remember several of these visits quite vividly. One morning I drove up to a large, old, run-down wooden house close to the central business district. I parked outside and without warning, notice or invitation opened the gate and walked along a narrow strip of concrete towards the front steps. A group of children playing in the yard stopped what they were doing, called out something about migloos and ran into the deep shade under the house and peered at me suspiciously from behind the wooden stumps. One child ran urgently up the back steps to tell the adults of my approach. When I climbed the front stairs and knocked on the door conversation inside stopped. After a brief period of silence there were rapid whispered exchanges. Eventually a man cautiously opened the door just wide enough to look out and see what I was doing there. He was extremely anxious. He was frightened of me. I might be a detective, or a government official or the landlord's agent. Why else would I be there? A white man wielded power. A white man meant trouble.

On another occasion, when walking through the gate into the front yard of another house, a little girl of about seven stood still in the middle of the path. She didn't move as I approached. She didn't say anything. She just looked up at me in a way that I have never forgotten. No child had ever looked at me like that before. There was a mixture of concern, anxiety and distaste. It wasn't particularly personal. But it was even more disturbing because of that. She looked at me across a wide gulf of suspicion and distrust. I was a migloo and she didn't like me or want me in her yard. I carried with me a history that I still had to learn about. Other events drove this lesson home.

One Sunday afternoon we were walking along the beach with children and dog. A young Aboriginal man approached us a little further up the beach. As he drew level with us he took two quick steps and kicked the dog with great force. The dog yelped and scampered away. We were transfixed, shocked into silence. The kick was so calculated, so deliberate. Its symbolic meaning was brutally clear. On another occasion I was confronted by a young Aboriginal man who stopped me in the street. He was very drunk; his glance was unguarded. He put a hand on my shoulder, staring intently at me. He didn't say a word; nor did he need to. His brown eyes were riveting, brimming with overpowering emotion, with hatred and contempt. Once again it wasn't particularly personal. It was ancestral and it was awful. It was also a history lesson of the most powerful kind, more telling than any amount of research in the archives. For that long moment I embodied the saga of conquest. I was held responsible for the past. I was a migloo and I was implicated. As the young man gripped my shoulder I was gripped with fear, expecting any moment to be attacked. I relived and understood the terror that so often and so widely ran like a powerful current beneath the surface of settler societies all over the world.

Confron

Doubts about the ability of Europ

increased anxiety and uncert

1941–43 and dark rumours

Line appeared to be a fu

During the nine

with Chinese, Ja

pioneers. W

times fe

rem

While Aborigines a ⟶ ...p̶.̶.̶.̶.̶ ̶ ̶ ̶.̶.̶ their bitter history of loss and oppression, white North Queenslanders wished it buried and forgotten. And forgetting was not difficult in a community with its eyes and mind set resolutely on the future and which had a highly mobile population. Families came north, stayed a while and then moved on. History did not rate highly among them. There were no local museums, few historical societies, few monuments to past events. Memorabilia were often lost or damaged in floods or cyclones or attacked by insects, or mouldered away in the heavy humidity. Even the towns had an air of impermanence about them. And yet the past bore down on North Queenslanders whether they knew it or not.

Racism had left a powerful legacy. The community had long felt itself both isolated and vulnerable, far away from the white Australian heartland, too close to the vast populations of Asia. Anxiety about uncontrollable migration in the nineteenth century was replaced in the twentieth century by fear of invasion.

eans to thrive in the tropics
ainty. The Japanese threat of
about retreat to below the Brisbane
ilment of long-held fears.

teenth century, settlers had shared the north
panese and Melanesian migrants. They too were
hile the dense Aboriginal population of pre-contact
l dramatically with the arrival of the settlers, there
ained a substantial indigenous population in all districts.
rontier fears of Aboriginal attack were replaced by anxiety
about racial mixture, the dilution of white blood and the growth
of a half-caste population.

The north provided an ideal environment for the propagation
of social Darwinism. The concept of race and the attendant idea of
social evolution were eagerly embraced on the frontier as both
intellectual explanation and moral justification for the drive to
establish a white Australia. The brutal work of pioneering was
associated with the most important scientific thinking of the age.
Social Darwinism could be used to justify the dispossession of
the Aborigines, the exclusion of non-European migrants and the
expulsion of the Melanesian labourers in 1906. Ideas which so
neatly fitted local circumstances and which underpinned local
prejudices were not easily surrendered. They persisted longer in
the north than in metropolitan Australia and are not entirely sup-
planted today. North Queenslanders may not have had much
interest in old things, but old and convenient ideas were another
matter altogether.

When, in the 1950s and 1960s, attitudes to race began to shift,
change took place unevenly – moving more quickly in the cities
and in the south than in the provincial towns and in the north,

where fewer people had higher education or access to the metropolitan media. The movement to reform the White Australia
Policy had little apparent impact in the north. The small resident
Chinese-Australian community was an accepted part of the local
scene, but the appearance of self-confident and obviously pros-
perous Asian visitors was clearly upsetting for many people. I
can remember one morning when a party of young Asian men
walked down Flinders Street talking and laughing loudly. The
older people – men and women alike – looked aghast. They
were both surprised and hostile. Soon after I arrived in Townsville I went on a speaking tour of western Queensland to explain
why I thought it was necessary to admit non-European migrants
and get rid of the White Australia Policy. In one small pastoral
town there was little interest at all in my lecture. My audience in
the School of Arts hall comprised the local schoolmaster, who
was my host, his small son, an old man and his dog. As I delivered
my piece the old man went to sleep and snored, the dog was sick
under the chair and the small boy looked bored beyond measure. In the next town I had a captive, but hardly appreciative,
audience, because my grazier host took me to the monthly
meeting of the Lions Club. After dinner, after club business
and associated roars from members, I rose to speak. But as I
laboured through my speech I sensed that the audience wasn't
really with me and I sat down to perfunctory applause. The first
and only question I was asked was: 'So what are these Asians
going to do when they get here, eh? Climb back up into the
trees?' I was lost for words. The audience grinned in triumph. I
had been put in my place.

In Townsville the local expert on racial questions was an old
man who owned a private ethnographic museum. He spoke and

wrote with great authority because he had once edited a leading anthropological journal in Sydney. In letters to the local papers he defended the White Australia Policy in the name of racial purity. In a letter of July 1971 entitled 'Mongrelization', he declared that the battle was on between 'mongrel supporters and White Australia'. He called on the community to stand up for a white Australia, 'as did the pioneers that opened up this continent for the great white race'. History, he believed, was on his side. The Roman Empire became 'integrated with lesser breeds and . . . declined into a rabble'. Britain was in contemporary decline because it had become 'partly mongrelized by the Pakistanis, West Indian negroes and others'. In another letter, entitled 'Racists v Mongrelists', he declared that from the earliest times 'practically all great men were pure breeds' and the same held true for the present day. In a sweeping conclusion he wrote:

> Everyone who has the interests of our country at heart should be proud of being a White Australian, and oppose the mongrelists controlled from outside Australia who are trying to soften us up prior to unloading some of the British Commonwealth's horrible mixtures on to us.

The old ethnographer was equally emphatic about Aboriginal Australians. Full-bloods had an integrity and nobility. Half-castes were degenerate, inheriting the worst qualities of both races. There could never be racial equality because Aborigines had much smaller brains than did Europeans. They were biologically incapable of emulating the white race.

Townsville was also home to retired pastoralists who spoke of how they 'knew the blacks', having worked with them for many decades on stations in the vast hinterland. One such pioneer wrote to the local paper explaining that he had 'spent all of this century and part of the last among the Aborigines and I believe I have acquired some understanding of them, their weaknesses and their strengths'. But he was convinced of inherent Aboriginal inferiority. He observed that Albert Schweitzer had said: 'The Negro is a child and with children nothing can be done without the use of authority'. The old pioneer claimed that although Africans had a brain cavity which was 15 cubic centimetres smaller than the average white man's, they were intellectually 'far above the Australian full-blood Aboriginal', who was quite unable to cope in competition with the white man and could never become an equal citizen of the country.

The ethnographer and the old squatter were men of their time. They had grown up when few people questioned the primacy of race. What was more disturbing was that many younger people agreed with their views. Margaret got a mixed reception when she approached the local primary schools to see if there were Aboriginal or Islander children who could take part in an art competition. One young headmaster of a school with a considerable number of indigenous children was quite enthusiastic. He said the 'darkies' were lovely kids. They were good at both art and sport. But he did not expect much from them academically because they had smaller brains than European children. He spoke sympathetically, in confidence and with complete certainty.

We realised soon after arriving in the north that almost every white person we met had views about the blacks and was confident in his or her knowledge and understanding of the subject. People who would not venture an opinion about anything else would speak openly and often about Aborigines and Islanders. No special knowledge or experience was necessary. Everyone, it seemed, could come up with anecdotes – second, third, fourth or fifth hand – which were thought capable of proving any point or winning any argument. There was a rich and dense folklore which defied logic and rebuffed rational argument. It was deployed most effectively against outsiders and visitors, who could be assailed as ignorant and unaware of local realities. During the 1960s and 1970s people unselfconsciously used epithets such as 'coon', 'boong', 'nigger' and 'abo' in every-day conversation without concern about meeting disapproval from their listeners. Racist jokes were also popular and were told and retold with minor variations.

One incident is still fresh in my mind. We were out to dinner at a recently opened French restaurant. It was the first such place in town and was usually a venue for amiable and subdued conversation. As we ate we became aware of loud talking at a nearby table. There were four couples, who were probably in their thirties and who looked as though they might be teachers or public servants. One couple was either visiting from the south or had just arrived in town to take up new jobs. The conversation was about the Aborigines. In itself that wasn't unusual. After a round or two of racist jokes the locals began to outline the ways in which they would 'get rid of the blacks', ranging from segregation through sterilisation to annihilation. Some of their projected schemes were highly elaborate and horribly inventive. The southern couple were obviously uncomfortable and looked anxiously around to see what the other diners were thinking. They clearly didn't know how to respond and whether they should laugh at the jokes or not.

In retrospect it seems as though the whole performance may

have been for their benefit. It was a display of racist bravado aimed at initiating the southerners into the ways of the north. It was a process that had probably been repeated many times before. Newcomers were confronted with racist language and attitudes and were presented with the dilemma of complicity or confrontation in circumstances where they could be persuaded that they lacked local knowledge or understanding. The choice was to go along with new friends or colleagues or to risk causing serious offence and be viewed as eccentric or self-righteous or to be assuming moral superiority.

I realise now that I was fortunate that it was a situation I was never forced to deal with. The University College was a totally new institution with very few links with North Queensland's past. Almost everyone who worked there had recently arrived either from overseas or from the southern states. The crude racism of the type expressed around the table in the French restaurant would have been regarded as offensive in university gatherings, although this was not necessarily the case with some members of the local support group which had successfully agitated for the foundation of the university. While overt racism was unacceptable, there was clearly a feeling that too much enthusiasm in the Aboriginal cause was imprudent and possibly damaging to the college's standing in the community.

But deeply disturbing things happened or comments were made at times when they were least expected. I remember clearly an incident which took place at a private dinner party. I was sitting next to an able, progressive young lawyer. He was a man of concern and compassion. Late in the night, as we talked about race relations, he confided in me that no matter how hard he tried he could not bring himself to believe that killing a black man was as serious a matter as killing a white one. He was deeply disturbed about this but ruthlessly honest with himself. I didn't know what to say in response to such shocking candour. Practically everything else about the night – who else was there, whose place we were at, what else was said – has faded from my memory. His confession will remain with me forever as an illustration of the way in which, in Queensland, attitudes shaped in the colonial period lived on into the present.

I have often wondered why I didn't take issue with people on this and many other occasions and press my own opinions, confront them, denounce their comments or jokes or arguments as racist. From the earliest days in Townsville I was much more likely to make some noncommittal comment, let the matter drop or actually draw the other person out and find out more about their views and why they held them. I'm not sure whether this avoidance of personal confrontation was due to cowardice, a prudent avoidance of engagement, or politeness inculcated long ago in childhood. I knew people who acted in a contrary way, who denounced racism wherever they heard it, taking on all and sundry in the process. I admired their courage and zeal but felt no urge to emulate them.

Once Margaret and I became known in the community as pro-black zealots, people who recognised us were inclined to adopt contradictory courses of action. Either they went out of their way to avoid any reference to racial matters at all, or they took the opposite path and endeavoured to provoke us by telling the latest racist joke or relating the most recent fragment of urban folklore about Aboriginal privileges or delinquencies.

The term racist seemed quite inadequate to cover the range of views and opinions we encountered or the jumble of often contradictory views people held at any one time. It was clear that many North Queenslanders were still influenced by the ideas they had imbibed in childhood. They had been brought up to believe that race was a fixed biological category, that Europeans and Aborigines were separated by unchangeable physical and cultural characteristics and that Aborigines were Stone Age people who had not advanced as Europeans had along the ascending path of cultural and social progress. Such ideas had pervaded Australian life until the 1940s or 1950s and many people continued to cling to them through their life and would no doubt take them to the grave. While views of this kind could be easily labelled racist, that categorisation did not on its own provide an understanding of the problem. They did not necessarily lead people to act or speak with hostility towards indigenous people. Indeed, they often coexisted with sympathetic interest and a desire to lend a helping hand, inspired by the conviction that the Aborigines were a unique and special people who should be assisted in every possible way and whose culture was worthy of respect. People with such views did not consider themselves racist and would have strenuously rejected that characterisation and been deeply offended by the imputation.

At the same time, there were racists who were hostile and truculent and who openly pronounced their hatred for indigenous people and often for other non-Europeans as well. They saw the world in terms of racial superiority and subordination and feared racial mixture. They were activists who were as often as not driven by inner anger about the world around them. They advocated direct action and were determined to 'keep the blacks in their place'. I found such racial activists frightening and dangerously unpredictable. They had contempt for 'nigger lovers', viewing them as turncoats and traitors to their race.

Race was an inescapable moral, political and psychological challenge in North Queensland. It could not be avoided. It was impossible to change one's appearance or skin colour or to shed one's race. In that way race was very different from social class, the characteristics of which were acquired and could be learnt and therefore modified by slight adjustments to accent and vocabulary, gesture and stance. Tasmania provided a good schooling in the subtle gradations of class and status, and the ways to manoeuvre up and down the hierarchy. But race was another matter altogether. The fact of being white, of being a migloo, was inescapable and it was unchangeable. One's opinions and attitudes were irrelevant. Whiteness was an inherited, unearned asset. In North Queensland it made life much easier, but it also meant being instantly judged by black Australians, being categorised and assessed in advance, being viewed not as an individual but as a member of a race. On the other hand, whites assumed a mutual identity, a community of interest, a deep unspoken complicity.

Coming into a racially divided society with good and no doubt naive intentions towards the Aborigines, we went out of our way to display our lack of prejudice, our colourblind virtue. This often involved assuming a form of inverse racism – automatically taking the Aboriginal side in public debate, speaking not just of them but for them. It was no doubt a better way to proceed than being prejudiced against Aborigines and always assuming the worst of them. But it was prejudice none the less. It clouded judgement and led to special pleading, double standards and a measure of hypocrisy, although we didn't realise that at the time. Eventually, experience undermined simple attitudes and ready-made answers. We met so many Aborigines and Islanders in so many different situations that generalisations became harder to articulate. It became obvious that there was almost as much variety and no greater virtue in the black community than there was in the white one. Increasingly, the individual personality came to seem more important than the collective identity. While experience gave us a much more nuanced view of race, it did not diminish our political commitment to the Aboriginal cause.

The psychological conflict produced by race ran deep and remained there even when it had been resolved in the conscious mind. It emerged in dreams. For a number of years I had a series of recurring dreams. Three I still remember. One was set in the house on the hill where we spent our first three Townsville years. It was a classic timber Queenslander, standing on low stumps with wooden shutters set in the walls below the windows to provide for the maximum amount of draught. It was night-time in the dream. A group of Aborigines was outside in the dark. They gathered under the open shutters, caught in the light. They pressed their faces against the shutters, staring into the house, reaching in. Their hands came right into the house. They were deeply threatening.

The second dream was set in the garden. I was standing with a group of Aboriginal men. Somehow my contact lenses had come out and fallen onto a concrete path. Sometimes one man, sometimes several, stamped on them despite my protests and anguish. The men were often strangers to me. Sometimes I knew who they were. One was my friend Eddie Mabo.

As I researched the violent colonial frontier, fragments of my research began to intrude into my dreams in strange and worrying patterns, in agitated scenes of turmoil, gunfire and sexual violence. Sometimes I was an observer looking on from some detached vantage point almost as a historian does when reading about the past. But on other occasions I seemed to be involved, with violence swirling all around me. It was probably fortunate that I could usually only recall scraps of the dreams when I woke – no more than troubling hints of nocturnal mayhem. But there was one vivid dream that I did remember and now can't forget. It was set in my family home in Hobart – or rather in the backyard, which we called the drying ground. When I was young there was an old walnut tree close to and overlooking a high paling fence, the other side of which was a vacant paddock half covered in gorse. In the middle of the paddock there was an old round galvanised-iron tank. My brother and his friends had a tree house and used to have pitched battles with a group of boys from around the neighbourhood who had turned the tank into their fort. The two belligerent parties exchanged a lethal fire of stones – both thrown and projected from homemade shanghais. I was small in this season of epic battles and was left on the ground to find stones in the garden and on the paths and to pass them up to the warriors in the tree house.

In my dream I was up in the tree house. I was so pleased to be there. I was standing next to a shadowy figure – I'm not sure who – and we were battling a hostile group in the paddock. But we were shooting rifles and fired every time heads appeared above the rim of the tank.

There were two deeply disturbing things about the dream. As our bullets hit home I could hear the noise they made, an utterly distinctive, terrible sound. It was a sound I had never really heard – not in my waking life – but a sound that I will never be able to forget.

There was a second shocking thing about the dream. Some hours after I woke and recalled its main outline it came to me in a sudden startling flash of memory. It was about the men in the tank. The heads, arms and upper torsos that I shot at were black.

As troubling as the dream was, it probably had a salutary effect, curbing my tendency to self-righteousness, dampening down my sense of self-evident virtue where matters of race were concerned, alerting me to how deeply such prejudice was embedded in almost any Australian of my generation, how pervasive images of the imperial frontiers had been in the books I read and pictures I looked at in my childhood.

Disturbing dreams and violent sentiments were not as shocking as brutal acts. North Queensland society was much more violent than either Tasmania or London.

Individuals were routinely more aggressive in manner, gesture and speech. Every time we returned after holidays in the south our awareness of it was renewed. At times, latent violence seemed to be in the air itself like electricity waiting for a storm. Fighting was accepted as both a spectator and a participatory sport. I'm sure we saw more street brawls in our first year in Townsville than we had seen in our life before. Many were inter-racial fights which broke out in the pubs, and frequently burst through the swing doors and onto the adjacent footpath and roadway. Because we walked into town and back every day along lower Flinders Street with its four rough pubs, we became adept at skirting warily around the unpredictable mêlées. But one morning Margaret could not avoid getting involved.

She was pushing the pram up Flinders Street and heard shouting as she approached the first of the four hotels. As she was passing the door into the front bar two white men emerged, dragging a struggling Aborigine. They threw him across the footpath just in front of the pram. His head struck the gutter with a sickening thud. He lay dazed by the impact and blood poured from a gash in his scalp. Two-and-a-half-year-old John said, 'Look, mummy! Poor man.'

Margaret left the pram and pushed through the swing door into the bar. There were whistles and catcalls from the early-morning drinkers. Women didn't venture into bars in North Queensland in those days. She called out to the barman, 'Quick, call an ambulance! A man outside has been badly hurt.' The barman replied, speaking more to the drinkers than to Margaret, 'This sheila wants to help that drunken black bastard.' Everyone in the bar laughed. No-one did anything except to resume the whistling and catcalling. She retreated, took hold of the pram and ran up the street to the post office and rang the ambulance. When she explained what had happened and that a man was lying injured on the footpath, the ambulance officer asked if he was black. When she replied that as a matter of fact he was, the officer showed no interest at all in the case. She then called the police. They took the matter seriously and asked her for details. They said they would be in contact with her in case it was decided to press charges and they needed her to make a statement. She heard nothing further from them.

It was not always a case of whites starting fights with blacks and beating them up. Aborigines picked fights with hapless whitefellas who were minding their own business and just wanted to be left alone. One lone drinker was king-hit by an Aborigine standing near him who, when taken to court, could offer no explanation at all for his assault. On other occasions the cause of the violence emerged in evidence, as in the case of a Torres Strait Islander who bashed a white man in the park on the seafront; the white man died later in hospital. The two had been drinking together during the day. It turned out that the white man had tried to shoot the Islander in the Northern Territory twenty years before. He kept laughing and joking about it and boasted that he had already shot eight blackfellas. In court the Islander explained why he had bashed his drinking companion: 'When we got down in the park he started talking about it, so I gave him a good hiding to teach him not to shoot at blacks . . . I punched him like he was a punching ball.'

At some pubs, a tradition of brawling developed in which each assault or fight was blamed on the previous one. There were always outstanding scores to settle, bruised bodies or bruised egos to avenge. This was often the case in conflicts between the young Aboriginal men and the soldiers who began arriving at the new army base late in 1966. For years afterwards the town was alive with rumours of bashings, brawls, cracked skulls, even crude castrations. It was impossible to find out how much truth there was in the rumours. But they were by no means improbable.

Although Aborigines often gave as good as they got, the spectators at fights were usually white and were often vicariously engaged in the conflict, cheering on the white combatants as though they were carrying out some collective mission, expressing shared hostility and hatred. There was an intensity and close togetherness about the crowds that was very striking. I remember one such fight that I came on by accident. It was outside a pub on a median strip. Two white men were grappling with an Aborigine. One behind was trying to hold him steady enough to allow the one in front to deliver a telling blow. As the

Aborigine bent over to protect his face, the assailant in front was trying to bring up his knee and smash it into the down-turned face. The watching crowd became increasingly excited waiting for the king hit. When the knee finally thudded into the face the crowd roared with delight. There were cries of 'Gotcha' and 'Got him' and 'Take that, you black bastard'.

The hotels were focal points of conflict in the 1960s and 1970s. For the first time there were significant numbers of Aborigines and Islanders living in town and prohibitions on serving them alcohol had been removed as a result of legislation passed in 1965. White male drinkers sought to preserve their exclusive possession of the bars. Many hotel managers, bowing to their patrons' prejudices, refused to serve blacks. Sometimes they simply declared that indigenous people were not admitted; more often they used some other excuse relating to dress, or accused would-be drinkers of being troublemakers. Aborigines were burdened with responsibility for what other Aborigines had done in the past.

Pubs which admitted black patrons attracted more indigenous drinkers and for a season became known as 'the abos' pub' with a consequent decline in white patronage. Policy would change after some bad incident, a complaint from the public or the arrival of a new manager. Indigenous drinkers were turned away and the whole process would begin again.

One afternoon Margaret and I were invited to meet a new proprietress who had opened a restaurant in a Flinders Street hotel and wanted to show it to us. She was hoping to upgrade the image of the establishment. The dining room was pleasantly decorated, although a little too genteel and not particularly appropriate for the tropics. As we exchanged pleasantries her husband came in to meet us. He was a very big man, an ex-rugby player with forearms as thick as his thighs. He too had a mission to change the image of the pub, which had a considerable Aboriginal clientele. He explained that the brewery had sent him to Townsville to clean up the place. It was then he showed us his big freckled fists. They were covered with cuts and bruises. He said that it had taken him a week to clear the blacks out of the front bar and to make sure they wouldn't come back.

Individual drinkers took on the same task themselves, as Eddie Mabo once discovered. He had stopped at a drive-in bottle shop on his way home. As he walked towards his car he was confronted by two young white men who walked up to him and said, 'There is no place in this hotel for you, nigger,' and punched him in the face, breaking his nose. Eddie took down the number of his assailants' car and reported the incident to the police but they never took any action, despite numerous enquiries as to what progress was being made.

In the 1970s it was clear that the police saw themselves as partisans in racial conflict. The Superintendent of the Cairns police told a North Queensland television audience that his men had to use tough measures against the blacks. People should understand that the force was 'holding down 30 000 of them'. There is considerable evidence to suggest that crimes committed against Aborigines were not treated as seriously as those directed at whites. A friend of ours heard a woman crying in the street outside his home. He found an Islander woman in deep distress. She had been raped. He took her inside, called the police and explained what had happened. The response surprised him. The first question they asked was 'Is she black?' When he said yes, any sense of urgency evaporated.

But much of the worst public violence was that which took place within the indigenous community. The groups living out in the parks and on the beaches and waste ground displayed both a strong collective sense of camaraderie and a propensity for extreme violence. In episodic brawling men and women were kicked unconscious, had faces and heads and arms terribly lacerated with broken bottles, or had legs and arms broken. Every so often one of the 'parkies', as they came to be known, died as a result of such violence. Much of the violence took place in the open in full view of people driving or walking past.

It was not easy to know what to do when faced by shocking public violence. Like most people, most of the time we skirted around the mêlées with averted eyes, not knowing what else we could do. But occasionally such detachment was hard to sustain. Late one night we were woken up by the most horrifying screams right outside our gate. Two women were being bashed by their male companions. It sounded as though they were being killed. After listening indecisively for a few minutes with the screaming getting louder, Margaret, unwilling to passively listen while the women were being brutalised, rang the police. The altercation continued until the police arrived. As soon as they got out of the patrol car and slammed the doors the four Aborigines forgot their own differences and turned on the police. After a short intense brawl the Aborigines were forced into the paddy wagon with the obvious possibility of their being roughed up when they reached the watch-house. I have often wondered since if we did the right thing and I'm still not sure even now.

The parkies were always a cause of controversy, a focal point for anti-Aboriginal rhetoric, an ever-present means to condemn the whole indigenous community. Racists could use the violence and squalor of the camps to whip up anti-Aboriginal sentiment. Everyone who was black was held responsible for a small minority, many of whom were alcoholics. Public outrage was even more vociferous when occasional attacks were made on passing whites or on tourists. Opposition politicians demanded action of local, state or federal governments, calling for the clearing out of the parkies. When public figures raised the temperature of the debate, angry individuals felt empowered to take vigilante action. Shots were fired from passing cars over the heads of sleeping camp-dwellers. Occasionally petrol bombs were thrown into the camps. This caused considerable public concern, but no-one was ever arrested for such action. And some people found humour in the grim situation. Soon after one petrol-bomb attack the popular hosts of a local theatre-restaurant told their audience a joke which ran:

'My mate Johnno is not happy with his petrol consumption.'
'Why, what's the matter?'
'He can only get two boongs to the gallon.'

Not everyone in the audience laughed.

VI

Becoming Involved

While still in England we had decided we would 'do something for the Aborigines' when we arrived in Townsville. I don't think we had any idea as to what the something might be or how it could be achieved. Up till that time we had no experience of activism. As a student I had been more interested in politics than had Margaret and had helped form what we called the Radical Society at the University of Tasmania. It had a brief and not especially distinguished history. Our most notable achievement was to bring the sacked philosophy professor Sydney Sparks Orr back to the university to give a lecture commemorating the centenary of the publication of John Stuart Mill's famous essay on liberty. But politics was something I talked, and no doubt pontificated about. I never actually *did* anything apart from voting.

In Townsville we became activists. Our first cause was the Vietnam War. We had heard of Australia's commitment of troops while in London, where the war was not popular and where the media assessment of the conflict was much more critical than in

Australia. We arrived back already opposed to Australia's involvement. Our activities varied widely in style and respectability. In
August 1966 I established a North Queensland branch of the
Australian Institute of International Affairs. The local National
Civic Council (NCC) and Democratic Labour Party (DLP) were
highly suspicious. They knew a communist front organisation
when they saw one. The word 'international' was an obvious
giveaway. But they joined to keep an eye on things. Consequently
our meetings were like miniature cold wars. As a very inexperienced president I tried to remember what I had read in a recently
purchased book on meeting procedure in order to contain the
conflict. But despite the contention, the Institute provided a
valuable forum for public discussion of international relations in
general and the Vietnam War in particular. There was an urgency
and intensity in the local debate because from early in 1967 the
new Lavarack Barracks on the edge of town became a forward
training base for troops going north into the battle zone.

Both Margaret and I joined the local anti-war Peace Committee, which brought together radical clergymen and members
of the small but influential Communist Party. There were times
in 1966 and 1967 when our big kitchen seemed half full of
clergymen. Margaret branched out on her own soon after on an
even less respectable path. She had read in the paper of the
women's anticonscription organisation 'Save Our Sons' and
decided to form a local branch, which came to life in a blaze of
publicity. Most of the other members were activists from the
Union of Australian Women and wives of Communist Party
union officials. The group collected signatures on petitions,
sampled public opinion and managed to attract publicity which
belied its small size. In the manner of the times, the formation of

Save Our Sons was reported on local radio as being the work of a Mrs Henry Reynolds, wife of a Townsville University College lecturer!

This did not endear us to many at the college, nor did the company we kept or the causes we espoused. Up until then there had been a very cosy relationship between town and gown. Most of the local elite were members of the Townsville and District University Society, which had done much to establish the college. They felt it was their institution. The first professors were social lions. They joined Rotary and were the most sought-after dinner guests for aspiring hostesses. A professor at table was a sign of social success. Our involvement in radical politics, our association with the communists, was seen as letting the side down and undermining the standing of the college. We received a chilly reception at social gatherings and I have no doubt the university administration was urged to pull us into line. It is to their credit that they didn't attempt to do so.

But more pressing and more constant than episodic social ostracism was the hostility we attracted from the very active local branches of the NCC and the DLP, members of which we regularly jousted with at public meetings and in the local media. They no doubt saw us as dupes of the Communist Party, but dangerous ones because we were articulate and brushed up well and were associated with the university.

We also suspected that our activities were attracting the interest of either the Special Branch of the Queensland police or the Australian Security Intelligence Organisation (ASIO), or both. Like many activists at the time, we swung from worrying about the situation to thinking that we were being paranoid about the whole question. Margaret had confirmation of ASIO's interest in her Save Our Sons branch many years later, when she was asked to give a lecture to politics students about her activism during the Vietnam War. After the lecture, a mature-age male student approached her and in conversation revealed that he had been asked to monitor her anticonscription activities in the 1960s. She was, or course, rather sceptical – yet he knew a great deal of detail about her, and subsequent discussions with a senior university staff member appeared to verify his claim.

It was also in 1966 that we became involved in Aboriginal politics. By chance, Margaret heard about an organisation called One People for Australia League (OPAL), a charitable group committed to the welfare of indigenous people. After attending her first meeting, Margaret returned home laden with minute books and correspondence files. She had been elected secretary at what turned out to be an annual general meeting, when the generally older membership were looking for youthful energy to promote their goals. Another young woman had also attended that meeting – Bobbi (Roberta) Sykes – and between them they certainly contributed to changes in OPAL (Townsville), the way it operated and the issues it raised.

However, Margaret and Bobbi did not appreciate that OPAL was ultraconservative and close to the right-wing National Party government. Its members were mainly elderly churchgoers who, while genuinely committed to improved opportunities for Aborigines and Torres Strait Islanders, were nevertheless totally absorbed in the assimilationist agenda of the day. They believed in giving a helping hand to 'their black brothers and sisters', and despite some radical initiatives we too became caught up in the prevailing mood of benevolence which marked the work of OPAL in the 1960s.

Bobbi and Margaret made quite a pair – they were stylish, striking in appearance and irreverent and both had a larrikin touch to their charm. They quickly teamed up and became the new public face of OPAL. Margaret's energy and efficiency had the almost moribund branch coursing with life and activity and it was all reported with great flair in the local media. But publicity had consequences we had not expected. Soon Aboriginal and Islander families were arriving on our doorstep seeking help at all hours of the day and night.

The reason for this needs some explaining. Aboriginal affairs in Townsville were run by the local director of the state DNA. The incumbent was a man of the old school who had been a highly authoritarian manager of Palm Island. He was seen by local Aborigines as 'very hard but very fair'. He also wielded enormous power and still had the ability to place people 'under the Act' and in effect exile them indefinitely to an Aboriginal reserve. While policy was changing rapidly at the time, old habits and old fears persisted. The director also dispensed charity. He provided housing for favoured families, he wrote out vouchers for free travel by train or by boat to Palm Island, and he provided orders for food parcels from local charities or stores.

It was only in 1966 that Aborigines and Islanders were given the same access to the welfare system as other Australians. My impression is that this had little immediate impact, as few indigenous families knew of their rights and there appeared to be no publicity to enlighten them. So they either depended on friends and relatives or turned to the state department with all its potential danger and threatening shadow of 'the Act'. OPAL was important because it provided another, non-threatening source of assistance with housing or food or transport. Other state agencies or local charities were often more inclined to refer people to OPAL than to the department. When all else failed, OPAL could be used as an indirect channel to solicit state government support. Once word got around that OPAL was back in business with a highly effective and sympathetic young secretary who lived on the hill in easy walking distance from town, we saw a steady procession of individuals and families seeking assistance.

The first family to appear was referred by the social worker at the Townsville General Hospital. A woman with several small children needed help to get back to a western town to visit relatives. She had just been released from the leper hospital on Phantome Island, a short distance from Palm Island, and had no support. None of the usual agencies would see her because they were frightened of leprosy. The social worker explained that there was nothing to worry about, but the word leprosy still evoked deep-seated fears. Margaret agreed to help, not without anxiety about two-year-old John, and the woman and her children duly arrived and spent an hour or so over a cup of tea. They then all set off down the hill to the DNA, which provided the required rail pass and a small amount of cash for the journey. News of the woman's medical condition had preceded her. She was made to wait outside the office while Margaret went in to press her case, but finally she and her family were able to board the Inlander.

Individuals and family groups sometimes turned up in a condition of complete destitution. They had often been sleeping out and arrived on the doorstep after having spent several days without food. On other occasions older people appeared who could scarcely walk, so sick that they required immediate medical attention. Women in the later stages of pregnancy who were sent from Palm Island to the hospital had no clothes to change into, no baby clothes at all, no nappies and no money to buy them. OPAL was called on to help, and Margaret was required to take the women to the Salvation Army or St Vincent de Paul to collect appropriate second-hand clothing.

Slowly but inexorably we were drawn into the existing system of paternalism, condescension and charity, and became increasingly uncomfortable with the situation. Margaret had to stand by while officials from the DNA spoke to Aboriginal men and women as though they were irresponsible and feckless children. The director of the department knew the intimate histories of all the Palm Island families and had access to records which detailed the history of any other person who had ever been 'under the Act'. He would talk to Margaret about families she was with as though they weren't there.

I became acutely aware of my own complex response to being directly involved as an agent of state government charity. At the time Margaret did not drive, so I often had to be the driver, courier and carrier. There was one such occasion that remains with me. A young Aboriginal woman and her daughter, whom we already knew, came to see us; she had run out of food and the DNA had given her an order for groceries at the general store in her suburb. She needed a lift, but she also had to have a white person to take the food order to the shop because she wasn't allowed to do this herself. So I drove her to the shop, handed over the voucher, and was told that I had to accompany her around the shelves to make sure she didn't waste any money on sweets, cigarettes or other non-essentials. It was either that or no food. I did what I had to do but was acutely embarrassed and shamed by the whole exercise.

We became, ourselves, dispensers of charity. People would

turn up at our home with unsolicited boxes of old clothes or toys saying they had brought them for the Aborigines. We often didn't know what to do with them. The toys were frequently broken, worn out or useless. But we realised the clothes might be of real assistance to many poor families. One box of clothes caused us considerable trouble. It had been left by a woman we had never seen before who said it was 'for the darkies'. We couldn't decide what to do with it. We felt we must do something, but decided that we couldn't very well take the clothes to one of the large charitable organisations, like the Salvation Army, given the conditions under which we had accepted them. Margaret asked me to deliver the box to one of the Aboriginal families in the city centre. I was reluctant to do so and kept putting the job off. She put the carton near the front door where I would remember it, but all to no avail. I resisted, but eventually she insisted. I stormed out of the house with the carton under my arm wondering whether I should dump it somewhere while saying that I had duly delivered it. I drove around for about twenty minutes in two minds, passing several possible houses on the way. Eventually I saw a woman sitting in her yard with her back to the road and her head in her hands. I stopped the car, picked up the box and moved quickly and self-consciously into the fenceless yard. I walked towards the woman, who half turned to see who was coming. Putting the carton down beside her I said, 'Here are some clothes for you.' Before she had a chance to respond I rushed back to the car blushing with embarrassment. I avoided driving past the house for several weeks after that.

Yet we did many things that were more constructive than dispensing solicited and unsolicited charity. One of the critical problems for indigenous people was employment. Many men found unskilled labouring jobs, but there was little work for women, and employers would not consider them for positions which involved dealing with the public. Margaret tried many approaches to break down these barriers, without success. But when a new Woolworths store in the city advertised a large number of positions she decided that a more direct approach was necessary. On the morning that interviews were to take place Margaret stationed herself by Woolworths' door and I began collecting mainly Torres Strait Islander women from nearby South Townsville and driving successive carloads over the bridge to Flinders Street. The management was completely thrown by this sudden visitation of Islander women in bright print frocks and with flowers in their hair. Margaret insisted that every woman receive an interview and helped them fill out their forms. The management went through the process, but not a single one of my passengers was offered a job.

Housing was another constant problem. There was a limited stock of public housing and the DNA placed 'reliable' families in houses under their control. Most other indigenous people had to rely on the private rental market. There were a small number of houses which the real estate agents designated as suitable for black families, either because of undesirable location or dilapidation. These were invariably overcrowded with large numbers of tenants, so it was a constant battle to try and get agents to place families in somewhat better housing. Margaret had many arguments with letting agents and many long conversations trying to ease the situation. Because her voice soon became known, the agents quickly realised who it was ringing about advertised property and reacted accordingly. Then there were occasions when landlords threw Aboriginal tenants out of their houses.

One night one of our friends was put out in the street with all her possessions. Margaret called the police and insisted that the landlord proceed in the appropriate manner, and watched with satisfaction as the police supervised the family's temporary reinstatement until they had received the required notice.

The most enduring aspect of our work with OPAL was the foundation of Kindergarten Headstart. Margaret taught intellectually disabled children in both Tasmania and London and had been head teacher of special schools in Devonport and within the state's major institution near New Norfolk. It was perhaps inevitable that she would attempt to provide indigenous children with preschool education and so bring her politics and profession together. At the time there was a strong focus on the need for compensatory education for children of minorities in the United States. The student organisation ABSCHOL organised homework classes for Aboriginal and Islander children and a local branch was active at the University College in Townsville.

Kindergarten Headstart began life as the OPAL playgroup in a church hall near the centre of town. Margaret had announced her plans in the media and set up that first morning, laying out toys and educational games, but only a few children from houses nearby attended. It took further discussion with indigenous families and the provision of transport to and from the church hall to allay the very natural suspicion towards the project. As word got around, more families decided to participate and soon it was necessary to organise a team of voluntary drivers. Within a year over thirty children were attending two days a week, with Aboriginal and Islander women becoming directly involved either with the children or with the management committee.

Headstart clearly provided Aboriginal and Islander children

with important early educational experiences and preparation for primary school. Children came from homes without toys or games or books. Many Islander children spoke an indigenous language or Torres Strait Creole at home, while Aborigines used non-standard English.

Raising money for the kindergarten was a constant problem. It was necessary to put an enormous effort into organising door-knock appeals and mobilising large teams of collectors. In Tasmania Margaret had been highly successful in raising money from the service clubs for her special schools. Handicapped children always touched members' hearts and tapped their pockets. She expected to receive a similar response in Townsville, but indigenous children were another matter altogether. She spoke to local service clubs, explaining the purpose of the kindergarten in preparing children for school and thereby enhancing their chances of success later in life. But the members were hostile. In question time she was asked why Aboriginal and Islander children should receive special treatment. All Australian children, they said, should be treated the same. To do otherwise was to adopt the policies of apartheid. There were no friendly comments or supportive questions. She left the meeting deeply depressed and without any money.

We experienced similar reactions a few years later when our friends Harry Penrith (subsequently known as Burnum Burnum) and Eddie Mabo decided to set up a Black Community School. We heard about the project one night when Harry came rushing in to our place. That was not unusual. He was constantly dropping in to report some new venture or enthusiasm for a political campaign, a reform initiative or a business venture. But this night his excitement was about education. He announced that he and

Eddie had decided to establish a community school for indigenous children and they wanted our approval and support, which
we readily gave. I had known for some years that Eddie was
unhappy with the education his children were receiving. They
had been among the first pupils of Kindergarten Headstart and
while they performed well when they went on to primary
school, he believed that, like other Murray Island children raised
in Townsville, they were losing their own language and cultural
traditions. The primary schools at the time were totally mono-
cultural in emphasis and assimilationist in practice. He was
deeply exercised about the possible disappearance of Meriam
culture within a generation, and made valiant attempts to revive
the observance of Island religions and seasonal festivals. He asked
me to open one elaborate festival in a churchyard in South
Townsville. Harry's enthusiasm arose because he understood
Eddie's fears. He had been raised in an orphanage, had not learnt
his language or cultural traditions and keenly felt the loss. He
prepared a manifesto for the school, which was:

- to give black children an alternative education more suited to
  their needs
- to involve children's parents and the community in these children's education
- to provide a satisfactory climate for the tuition of children
  who are academically oriented and motivated towards even-
  tual tertiary education
- to be a focus around which the black community can operate.

The document denounced traditional schools for failing indigenous children. It was logical, therefore:

for us to seek alternatives which are going to maintain and increase black confidence.

We are convinced that given the right environment in a situation where we can employ teachers of our choice, where for a particular part of their education our children can be taught traditional pursuits in dancing, singing, cooking, fishing, hunting, etc. as well as normal subjects then we know they will respond.

A storm of controversy arose over the community school when it opened in September 1973. The *Townsville Daily Bulletin* campaigned against it, running a headline: 'Doubts Surround Legality of New Community School'. The article quoted Education Department officials, who declared that the school was without either status or standing and was in breach of the Education Act. In addition, people attempting to entice children away from a state primary school and enrol them in an unauthorised school were technically guilty of an offence and risked prosecution. The conservative independent member for South Townsville in the Queensland parliament, Tom Aitkens, declared that the school was racist, was the work of the 'Red Element at James Cook University' and was illegitimately using Commonwealth funds.

The Minister for Education agreed with Aitkens and said he thought there was justifiable suspicion about the motives of those involved in setting up the school. His views were announced in a large headline on the front page of the *Bulletin*: 'Motives of Townsville's Black School Justifiably Suspicious'.

Opposition was voiced by prominent members of the Aboriginal community, especially those who had come from Palm

Island and who thought that segregated schooling was a retro-grade step. The school began, and remained, largely a Torres Strait Islander – or even a Murray Islander – initiative. Commu-nity debate raged for a week or two, with James Cook academics coming out in support of the school. Margaret and I wrote one of our numerous indignant letters to the *Bulletin* attacking the paper's crusade against the school:

> We write concerning your article on the Black Community School . . . which raises serious misgivings. It would be plain to even the most casual reader that you disapprove of the ven-ture. The article is indeed opinionated, prejudiced and ten-dentious. Such strong views would be unexceptional if they were to appear in an editorial or as signed commentary. What you provide is personal opinion masquerading as news . . .
>
> The views embodied in the article are all the more surprising considering the long-standing support you have accorded to the right of parents to choose the type of educa-tion they desire for their children and to opt out of the State system. The families concerned have acted as many minori-ties have for at least one hundred years . . . The basic issue is this . . . are Aborigines and Torres Strait Islanders to have the same rights as the Catholics, Anglicans, Greeks, Jews, etc., etc.? Your answer, an emphatic even hysterical no, hints at racism and thus must cause disquiet about your atti-tude to race relations in this area.

The school survived and we continued to provide what support we could. Margaret gave professional advice about staffing, teaching methods and equipment and monitored the children's progress.

Opposition to the Black Community School was nowhere near as intense as the hostility aroused earlier by a large conference on race relations organised in December 1967, to discuss the implications of the referendum of that year which removed discriminatory sections from the constitution and which was supported in Townsville by a very large majority. The conference was proposed by key union officials who approached the mayor to call a public meeting, which was attended by 120 people. A large and diverse committee was elected to plan a program of local research into indigenous housing, education and employment which would report to the conference, to be called 'We the Australians: What is to Follow the Referendum'. The committee of twenty-five included clergymen, academics, schoolteachers, small-businessmen and three Torres Strait Islanders. It also included three communist union officials, with Margaret as secretary and conference organiser.

The participation of the unionists was enough to convince many people that the whole thing was a communist conspiracy to provoke racial conflict. Opposition began in the NCC, and spread from there to the Roman Catholic and Anglican churches. The two bishops publicly denounced the whole proceedings and withdrew church support, although individual clergymen defied their instructions. The DNA became deeply concerned and the board of OPAL insisted that the Townsville branch disassociate itself from the suspect conference. Margaret and Bobbi Sykes were singled out for particular criticism as they had earlier sent money from OPAL Townsville to the striking Gurindji families at Wave Hill Station, an action which was highly objectionable in the eyes of OPAL's hierarchy. The local committee met and refused to accept direction from Brisbane, so Margaret and

Bobbi were expelled from the League. The local members resigned and OPAL Townsville ceased to exist, but not before strenuously and successfully resisting attempts by Brisbane to take over the kindergarten.

The Queensland Special Branch were involved, monitoring the meetings leading up to the conference, and police cars were stationed outside the conference venue, recording car registration numbers of participants. On the day after the seminar police cars parked outside Kindergarten Headstart to record the registration numbers of volunteer drivers. Weeks before the conference, the police raided our flat one afternoon when we were out and searched Margaret's papers. They took lists of committee members and those people who had already registered for the conference, as well as all the cheques that had come in to pay registration fees. Margaret reported the burglary to the police. We heard nothing for a few days until the police rather oddly handed the documents to a local Communist Party official, saying that they had been found in the street.

Despite the boycotts and the harassment, the conference was a great success. Three hundred people attended the addresses by the invited speakers, C.D. Rowley, Colin Tatz, Faith Bandler and Joe McGinness, and the well-organised program of workshops. The most striking aspect of the conference was the large attendance by Aborigines and Islanders, who came from many outlying towns and communities. They made up about 40 per cent of the overall audience. No conference in Australia up to that time had ever had such significant indigenous participation, in both the plenary sessions and the workshops.

At the final session a number of resolutions were passed.

They came out of the various workshops and are therefore a good reflection of the issues which were seen to be important by North Queenslanders at the time. The resolutions were:

- That this seminar recommends to the consideration of the Federal Government the formulation of a Federal Act along the lines of the Repatriation Act with a 'crash' education programme, finance for home and business ownership, 'soldier settlement' type schemes on the land; the Aboriginal and Islander peoples having a strong voice in writing and administering the Act.
- That this seminar calls on the Commonwealth and State Governments to take all necessary steps to grant wage equality and opportunity to all Aboriginal and Torres Strait Island people — male and female — together with full rights under all Industrial and Social laws; and that this seminar draws attention to the urgent need for a Pearling and Pearl Culture Industry award.
- That mineral royalties should be paid when minerals are mined on Aboriginal reserves and the proceeds paid into a trust fund to be used for the training and education of Aborigines and Torres Strait Islanders.
- That this seminar calls on the Queensland Government to make it unlawful to discriminate against Aboriginals and Torres Strait Islanders on racial grounds.
- That this seminar draws the attention of the Queensland Government to the need for providing more extensive opportunities for employment in industry of Aborigines and Torres Strait Islanders in the Northern part of the State.
- That this seminar recommends to the Townsville City Council that it consider a case for homes at pegged rents for Aborigines in co-operation with the State Government or by itself.

- That a Civil Liberties group be elected in local areas by the Aboriginal and Torres Strait Islanders community in order to marshal wide public support for such causes.
- That this seminar recommends to the Queensland Government that the title of ownership of the present Aboriginal reserves or missions be granted to Aborigines, such land to be administered by a Lands Trust similar to that established recently in South Australia. It is considered necessary that the title of ownership of such land be inviolable: that only Aborigines be permitted to lease any portion of such an Aboriginal mission.
- That the seminar calls upon employers and unions in North Queensland to assist in solving the Aboriginal and Islander employment problem and that Trade Unions give consideration to the acceptance of 'crash' courses for the training and acceptance of artisans – in particular men who have already acquired some skill but which is not adequate to secure their entry to jobs as skilled employees.
- That a committee be formed comprising representatives from local bodies in Townsville, Aborigines and Torres Strait Islanders, to investigate, and where possible to redress, cases of racial discrimination.
- That a committee be formed to deal with the problems of housing for Aboriginal and Island people in Townsville, the committee to be prepared to take all possible legal and other measures to eliminate overcharging, bad maintenance, and other abuses.

On re-reading the seminar's recommendations, I found to my surprise that one requested me to convene a select committee to consider the 'sponsorship and support of a research project on the integration of Aborigines and Torres Strait Islanders into the Townsville community'. I had forgotten all about it. I'm not sure the committee ever met. We certainly didn't initiate a research project on integration. But over the next eighteen months my own research effort moved from Tasmania to Queensland. I, too, was bringing my professional life into line with my political life.

VII

Teaching and Learning – about Race

Before I arrived in Townsville I had no idea which sort of history I would be expected to teach. I hoped it would be European, an enthusiasm fired by return visits to Florence and Rome prior to embarking from Genoa. I had bought a small library of books about European cultural history with the hope that I could teach my students about the Renaissance, the Baroque and Romanticism. I wanted to tell them of Donatello, Brunelleschi, Bernini and Caravaggio. But before my books had been delivered to Townsville I had been instructed that I was to introduce the college's first course in Australian history. I was unenthusiastic about the task and reluctantly began to read systematically through the small collection of Australian history in the library, preparing lectures for the following year.

I can't remember much about those first lectures, delivered throughout 1966 to two small classes – a daytime and an evening one. I'm sure they were quite conventional, with little that was new in content or innovative in style. I began Australia's story in

Britain, with the decision to send the First Fleet to Botany Bay. I dealt sparingly with the Aborigines. I said something about their relations with the early governors and certainly dealt quite thoroughly with Tasmania's Black War and the removal of the Islanders to Flinders Island. I very much doubt if I mentioned them again during the rest of the year.

My lectures reflected the state of Australian history writing at the time. The textbook for the course, *Australia: A Social and Political History*, had been set by the History Department in Brisbane and was edited by department head Professor Gordon Greenwood. It had contributions from five other distinguished scholars and was probably the most widely used textbook at the time. It had been sponsored by the committee appointed to celebrate the Jubilee of Federation in 1951, although it did not appear until 1955. By the time I used it, it had been reissued five times and was to be reprinted a further eight times between then and 1974.

One of the most striking features of Greenwood's book was that the Aborigines had almost completely disappeared from the story. They were mentioned four times, but only in passing. They did not even earn an entry in the index. In his chapter on 'The Pastoral Ascendancy, 1820–50', the economic historian R.M. Hartwell declared that in his designated period Australia had 'large tracts of empty grazing country awaiting occupation'. A little later he reiterated the point, explaining that:

> As a process of colonisation, the settlement was relatively uncomplicated: the continent was empty, for the unfortunate aborigines offered no serious economic or cultural opposition, and the colonisers were of one nationality.

I was able to change the textbook for 1967, but I don't think I did so because the Aborigines were absent from the text. Although the Greenwood book was the worst example of its kind, the other available general histories were little better. Five other major histories of Australia by established scholars published between 1954 and 1967 showed a collective desire to consider the 'Aboriginal question' as something which belonged to the early colonial period and had no modern sequel. All dealt with the Aboriginal policies of early governors, the Tasmanian Black War and conflict on the pastoral frontier in the 1830s. Only one author dealt with the second half of the nineteenth century and even then he confined his attention to Western Australia.

While becoming deeply engaged in contemporary racial politics, I continued to research and write about events in the colonial history of far-off Tasmania. My historical research and my everyday life drifted further and further apart. I looked at the convict system and its effect on island society after the cessation of transportation; I analysed the political power and social authority of large landowners; I assessed the importance of regionalism. I wrote papers and spoke at conferences on these topics in 1967 and 1968 and had three articles published in scholarly journals in 1969. They were my first academic publications and I was very proud of them.

My growing understanding of North Queensland society and of race relations, and my involvement with Aboriginal and Islander people, inexorably influenced the way I thought about the past and what I taught in my classes. Conventional Australian history provided little information either about North Queensland or about indigenous people. Both issues mattered to my students, who were practically all from the north. Some of them had never been anywhere else. Many of them were North Queensland patriots. And yet the history we studied had little to say about their own part of Australia, which had been settled after 1860 and seemed, therefore, to do no more than recapitulate earlier events which had occurred elsewhere. The pastoral occupation of the north was merely an extension of the squatting movement of the 1830s and 1840s in the south-east. The tropical gold rushes appeared to be a replay of the dramatic events on Victorian and New South Wales fields. Local students could be forgiven for thinking that nothing of importance had ever happened in their own part of the country, that history was something that had taken place 'down south', more than a thousand miles away.

North Queensland students also knew about race. They came from places where Aborigines, Torres Strait Islanders or Pacific Islanders were part of the community, and many had been to school with indigenous children. Even when this was not the case, they had been aware throughout their lives of the indigenous presence in North Queensland and the constant discussion and controversy about race in the white community. The issue mattered to them even while they differed widely in their opinions. Some students came from families which had promoted the Aboriginal cause. Others had grown up on remote cattle stations where black stockmen were the mainstay of the workforce. There were the children of teachers who had taught on Aboriginal or Torres Strait Island communities; sons and daughters of publicans who had to deal constantly with trouble in turbulent front bars. Some students arrived at the university bearing all the racist ideas abroad in the community. A few shed those ideas while they studied; others defiantly preserved them against challenge from teachers and fellow students.

When I began to speak more about race and the local history of violence and dispossession, the interest of the students was unmistakable. I was touching on local taboos. Sometimes it was possible actually to feel the collective emotional intensity. Some students retreated inside themselves, looking neither at me nor at their fellows. Others stared with ill-concealed hostility or exchanged complicit glances with like-minded friends. In those early years I was seen by many people as a troublemaking southerner, full of good intentions but ignorant of the way things were in the north. I remember one relevant incident quite vividly. I was returning essays to students in my office. An aggressive and tough young man came in. He was from a small country town in central Queensland. After doing our business we began talking about race. He was leaning on the other side of my small desk. He said, 'Yeah, we're very close to the blacks in our town.' As he spoke he half stood and leaned right across the desk. He smashed his closed right fist into an open left hand in front of my face, saying with venom, 'We're as close as that!'

But teaching about race was only part of a much larger project, which was to put as much local history as possible into general courses on Australian history. This involved setting aside three or four weeks which were devoted to North Queensland topics – the northern pastoral frontier and gold rushes, the maritime industries such as pearling and bêche-de-mer collecting, the sugar industry, the non-European migrants – Chinese, Melanesians and Japanese. Eventually our own students researched many of these topics and wrote theses, articles and books about them.

My first research student was a high school teacher called Noel Loos, who later became a colleague and wrote both a general history of white–Aboriginal relations in North Queensland and a biographical study of Eddie Mabo. He was in my first class in 1966 and then came to me looking for a topic for an honours thesis. I suggested he write a study of the impact of European settlement on Aboriginal society in the Bowen district, just south of Townsville. Bowen provided several advantages for such a project. The settlement was an official one and was consequently recorded from the first day. A local newspaper was published within a few years of settlement and the ship-wrecked English sailor James Morrell, who spent seventeen years living with the local Aborigines, left a short account of his life during that time.

It was through Noel that I had my first contact with the raw first-hand reporting of frontier conflict. It came as a shock, even though by then I had some idea of what to expect. The brutal frankness of contemporary debate was in such contrast to the avoidance and evasion of later historical accounts. Although I subsequently retraced my student's course through the local records, it was that first encounter with the discourse of the frontier which I will always remember. There was the matter-of-fact reporting of the actions of the Native Police in dispersing 'mobs' of Aborigines all over the district.

The Commissioner of Crown Lands and senior official in the new community wrote back to Brisbane six months after landing in Bowen, explaining that the Aborigines were:

> a race of bloodthirsty miscreants who believed in no God, nor in any spiritual power, who cannot even trust each other in their own domestic intercourse and who are enemies to all men until fear enforces submission.

Correspondents writing to the local paper, the *Port Denison Times*, talked openly about what was happening in the hinterland. The pioneer squatters adopted a course of action known as 'keeping them out', which involved never allowing the Aborigines on their stations: 'consequently they were hunted by anyone if seen in open country, and driven away or shot down when caught out of the scrub and broken ground'. This policy, one of the writers declared, was unavoidable, and quite necessary under the existing circumstances.

But even more chilling accounts found their way into the *Port Denison Times*, which, in June 1868, carried a report from the paper's Burketown correspondent about the activities of the local Native Police detachment under Sub-Inspector Uhr, whose:

> success I hear was complete. One mob of fourteen he rounded up, another mob of nine, and a last mob of eight, he succeeded with his troopers in shooting. In the latter lot there was one black who would not die after receiving eighteen or twenty bullets, but a trooper speedily put an end to his existence by smashing his skull . . . Everybody in the district is delighted with the wholesale slaughter dealt out by the native police, and thank Mr. Uhr for his energy in ridding the district of *fiftynine* (59) myalls.

In the same year a Bowen resident ruefully admitted in a letter to the paper, 'We know that our town at least had its foundations cemented in blood.'

All of this material was quite shocking. It was as if it was about another country, a violent, brutal place quite unlike the image of Australia that I had grown up with. I instantly and necessarily wondered how it was that I didn't know, why I hadn't been told in my schooling, why nothing I had read in the general histories had prepared me for the realities of pioneer settlement. Could this be how the frontier was everywhere?

As shocking as was the first acquaintance with the documentary evidence and casual acceptance of atrocity, the attitude of the Europeans to the Aborigines after the survivors had been 'let in' to Bowen was equally unexpected, equally disturbing. For the first time, I became aware of that compelling need to 'keep the blacks in their place' even when they were no longer a threat. In 1869 the editor of the *Port Denison Times* wrote a long article about the need to impose discipline on the Aborigines who were living in camps around the town. He commended the action of a local policeman who had stockwhipped a woman who stole a child's dress. While the action was not strictly legal, it was the right thing to do in the circumstances because it was essential to 'teach those principles of submission which our position renders it so necessary for us to enforce'. Hitherto the Europeans had done this:

> by the strong hand, that is to say, by unhesitating recourse to powder and ball. Against this system all right feeling men have thoroughly revolted and it has lately been hoped that the time has come when, with regard to our safety, a milder system might be inaugurated and more friendly relations established between us and those whom we have supplanted. How to effect this is the problem now before us and it is needless to say that it is by no means an easy one. In the first place of course it would be absurd under any circumstances to expect any kindly feeling to exist towards us in the breasts of the blackfellows especially so shortly after

the reign of terror by which they have hitherto been kept in subjection. In whatever plan we may adopt with respect to them we shall do well to bear in mind that their feelings towards us are and must be those of resentment and hostility and that however the exhibition of those feelings may be restrained by motives of policy on their part they do exist and probably will continue to do while the race lasts, and that this smouldering fire will be ready to burst into flame when favourable conditions offer.

Whilst therefore it is one of our foremost duties to escape as soon as possible from the terrible necessities which our position has forced upon us, we must not cease to be firm and must take especial care to show our black neighbours that whilst we are willing, nay anxious, to hold our hands from slaughter, we are at the same time determined to enforce at all hazards and by *any* means submission to our laws and that any infraction of them will be met by retribution prompt and severe.

It was powerful writing. It was also quite stunning for someone brought up on conventional stories about Australian history.

My students' pioneering research was only one of the ways in which I grew increasingly aware of Aboriginal history during 1967, 1968 and 1969. The more experience I had of race relations the more pressing was the need to understand how things had come to be the way they were. As we developed friendships with Aboriginal and Islander families, they felt confident enough in us to tell us the history of their kin – although at the time we didn't know enough of local history to put those stories in their proper context. A woman friend who often looked after our children told us how she had grown up on a mission run by a fundamentalist sect. She had been placed in a dormitory and had little contact with her parents and so was prevented from learning her language or anything about her culture. Her European education had been rudimentary. She had been subjected to rigid discipline. When an adolescent she was caught holding hands with a boy. She had her head shaved and was imprisoned in the dormitory. The boy was flogged with a stockwhip and sent away. Shortly before we met her, she had battled with the authorities to be given custody of her grandson, who had been taken away from her daughter. The daughter was subsequently brought before the court for a minor offence and, while acquitted, she was put under the Act and sent to a mission far away in the north. Some months later she died in childbirth before our friend could see her again.

Some time in late 1969 or early 1970 I decided to change the focus of my research from Tasmania to Queensland, from class to race, from convicts and free settlers to Aborigines. The decision had been advancing on me for a long time and, once made, opened the way for a period of intense reading and research. But it was made with some misgivings. There was little interest among senior historians in Aboriginal history. What had been written in the previous 30 years was the work of journalists, political scientists and anthropologists. I had no idea at the time that people in other parts of Australia were working on Aboriginal history. Writing in 1970, Charles Rowley observed that there were still historians who regarded Aboriginal affairs 'as not very important in the development of the Australian nation'. In some university departments there were scholars who thought there was 'something vaguely disreputable about such studies'.

A discussion I had with one of the most influential members of the profession was not encouraging. I had just given a paper on Tasmania at an academic conference and was asked what I was going to write about now I had gone to North Queensland. I rather tentatively said I thought I would do something about the Aborigines. My interrogator was dismissive, saying he didn't think 'there was much in that'. It set me back. When I returned to Townsville I sought out the opinion of my head of department, Brian Dalton. Fortunately and wisely, he advised me to pursue those issues which interested me.

My decision to do so was undoubtedly related to strong currents running through western society at the time, emerging from the American civil rights movement, anticolonial resistance, third-world nationalism and guerrilla warfare. But to some extent those issues took my attention beyond Australia into the wider world of international politics. Local events and local debate were decisive in determining my research plans. Some time late in 1969 I read the 1968 Australian Broadcasting Commission Boyer lectures which had been given that year by the celebrated anthropologist W.E.H. Stanner. The small book of the series was entitled After the Dreaming. They were brilliant lectures and they were enormously encouraging, confirming many ideas which were still only tentatively held. I was particularly stimulated by the second lecture in the series, entitled 'The Great Australian Silence', which was a sustained attack on the nation's historians. It helped strengthen my disquiet about mainstream historical writing. One passage in particular has remained with me ever since, and I've quoted it many times in lectures and articles. In referring to the lack of interest in Aboriginal questions among historians, Stanner observed that inattention on such a scale could not be explained by absentmindedness. He believed that it was a structural matter, 'a view from a window which has been carefully placed to exclude a whole quadrant of the landscape. What may well have begun as a simple forgetting of other possible views turned under habit and over time into something like a cult of forgetfulness practised on a national scale.'

Stanner pointed in the direction that my initial research took me – an examination of what historians and other writers had said about Aboriginal–European relations from as far back as the early nineteenth century. I read everything of relevance in the small university library and gave my first seminar on the subject in the history department in about May 1970.

The most striking thing to emerge from my reading was that in the nineteenth century the Aborigines had figured prominently in both historical and descriptive works. Almost universally they merited a chapter. In the major general histories they were treated seriously and at length. In Tasmania at least there had been a number of significant historical accounts of conflict between indigenous landowners and advancing settlers. The cult of forgetfulness was a more recent phenomenon, which emerged in the late nineteenth century and early twentieth century. It coincided with Federation and the flowering of Australian nationalism. A book which particularly interested me at the time was the official Jubilee history of Queensland, published in 1909. Although it was a long and detailed work, there was no mention of the Aborigines at all. Other works of the early years of the twentieth century celebrated 'the passing' of the Aborigines and saw it as proof of progress. Aboriginal society was a benchmark from which it was possible to measure white Australian advance. In her book *The Coming of the British to*

Australia, published in 1906, Ida Lee observed that among the scenes of progress it was difficult to realise 'that such people ever existed'. The black man, she declared, 'has all but passed away. His voice is never heard'. It was all for the good, she thought:

> But as we press forward let us turn to the few that remain and watch their vanishing figures. Let us ask, we who scattered them and who possess the country they so dearly loved, 'Is it well with the land?' The white townships growing where all was dark with forest; the axes ringing through the back-wood, the network of masts fringing the busy port; the golden corn colouring the grassy plains; the wealth of mine drawn from the barren waste, all unite in the full, clear answer 'It is well.'

With such views abroad in the community it is not surprising that the Aborigines began to 'vanish' from the historical works written to celebrate and define the new nation. But few writers were as frank about their intentions as the distinguished man of letters Walter Murdoch, who, in a book for children called *The Making of Australia*, published in 1917, declared that when people talk about the history of Australia:

> they mean the history of white people who have lived in Australia. There is a good reason why we should not stretch the term to make it include the story of the dark skinned wandering tribes who hurled boomerangs and ate snakes for long ages before the arrival of the first intruders from Europe.

The modern historian, Murdoch declared, was concerned with Australia only as the 'dwelling place of white men and women, settlers from overseas'. It was his business to tell the community how these white people 'found the land', how they settled it and explored it and how they gradually 'made it the Australia we [know] today'.

The more I read, the clearer it became that between 1900 and the 1960s the Aborigines were virtually written out of Australian history. 'The Great Australian Silence' settled over the new nation soon after Federation and was unbroken for over half a century. In 1959 the Professor of History at the Australian National University, J.A. La Nauze, delivered an address to his professional colleagues on the writing of national history during the 30 years between 1929 and 1959. He noted that lack of interest in the Aborigines was one of the distinguishing features of national historical writing, and marked it off from the stories told in other white settler societies for, 'unlike the Maori, the American Indian or the South African Bantu, the Australian aboriginal is noticed in our history only in a melancholy anthropological footnote'. La Nauze did not find this strange, nor did he suggest that it should be changed. In a general history of Australia published in 1962, Marjorie Barnard declared that history had made the Aborigines a 'codicil to the Australian story'. In 1966, the year I began lecturing, J.M. Ward, Challis Professor of History at Sydney University, published a study of the Australian colonies between 1840 and 1860 entitled *Empire in the Antipodes*. Although covering a period of massive incursion into Aboriginal territory, widespread frontier conflict, intense concern in the Colonial Office and vigorous debate in the colonies about race relations, the Aborigines are mentioned once – and then only in comparison with Maoris, who were a proud and warlike people who could not be 'relegated to obscurity in the same way as the aboriginals of Australia'.

In the course of my research I returned to Greenwood's *Australia* and saw it with new eyes. It was one of the last, and one of the most significant, products of the country's 'cult of forgetfulness'. But on reading the reviews published in the major historical journals in November 1955 I realised that this was still not a general view. None of the senior academics who assessed the book thought it strange that the great Australian silence still prevailed as intensely as it had ever done; none noticed the complete silence about the long history of white–Aboriginal relations.

Like many other young scholars around Australia at the time, I noted the Aboriginal relegation to obscurity with intense dissatisfaction which often enough erupted as anger at the cultural condescension and insensitivity it implied. Australia, we felt, had been badly let down by its historians. They provided no material, no analysis, no stories which would enable the community to understand the nature of contemporary relations between white and black Australians. The sudden emergence of Aborigines on the national political stage came without warning or prior reflection from historians. All this provided strong motivation to research and write and explain. There was a sense of urgency. We were self-appointed missionaries who were required to enlighten the public. If we raised our voices we felt that was necessary to shatter once and for all the great Australian silence.

In 1970, soon after I had completed my first paper on Aboriginal history, we went to England for study leave. In those far-off days Queensland academics were required to take their leave out of Australia. I had travelled from England to Australia in 1965 wanting to teach European history to my North Queensland students. Five years later I returned to London to spend six months researching Australian history in the Public Records Office and the wonderful library of the Royal Commonwealth Society, which had a comprehensive collection of material from the white settler societies. It was there that I found the books, journals and official papers which provided the material I used in the collection of documents published in 1972 as *Aborigines and Settlers*, the introduction of which expressed my views at the time about the history of race. The book, I explained, had been compiled in the belief:

> that the history of White–Aboriginal relations is important to Australians not only because it helps us understand the present, but because of all aspects of the past the fate of our [*sic*] coloured people demands the greatest expansion of our historical imagination. In the process we learn much about the dark underside of the Australian mind – the violence, the arrogant assertion of superiority, the ruthless single-minded and often amoral pursuit of material progress – those features so often hidden beneath the bland surface of coffee table historiography. If, as so often in the past, we exclude the Aborigines from our history, we may retain a flattering self image but we will scarcely develop a mature awareness of ourselves and our heritage.

Having returned to Townsville with bulging files of research notes, I was keenly aware that everything I had collected was a report, an account, a description written by Europeans. There were a few reports of what Aborigines had said and what they thought, but insufficient to provide any balance. With my two friends Noel Loos and Eddie Mabo, I set out to collect oral history from elderly Aborigines and Islanders in Townsville. We were totally inexperienced and had no appreciation of the finer points of the business, but we learnt as we went along and interviewed a wide range of men and women about their lives and experiences. We heard stories of hard labour, of poverty and oppression from people who had worked all their lives on cattle stations, on pearling and trochus luggers, on mission stations, on tin and gold fields. Many of our informants had stories handed down by their parents and grandparents about the arrival of the Europeans, about the killing times, sagas of sudden death and drawn-out deprivation.

Almost every story we heard brought the past to life in a way that few written documents could do. And many of the old people were wonderful storytellers. Perhaps the best raconteur was an old Torres Strait Islander whom we visited one hot night. He lived in a small wooden cottage. The garden was dominated by a large mango tree laden with fruit; bats fed and frolicked in the dark foliage, and the air was heavy with the sweet smell of rotting fruit strewn on the grass. The old man told us traditional stories from Murray Island. Many were about European shipwrecks and castaways. He spoke of the day in 1871 when the missionaries arrived. It was a story which had obviously been told and retold innumerable times before and re-enacted at the annual Coming of the Light Festival. Another old and detailed story concerned the arrival of a sailing ship which stood off the island. The local villagers lined the shore and could see the white men similarly lined up along the rails. The crew scrutinised the island, the islanders returned the gaze. The islanders noticed that one white man raised a telescope to his eye and scanned the beach. With great animation the old man stood up and said the Islanders could see the seaman looking at them with 'a white man's eye'. For a moment I imagined myself there on the beach with the Islanders. I felt that I stood on the other side of the frontier.

VIII

The Legacy of Terror

Violence was close to the surface of society in North Queensland thirty years ago. It took many forms and found many outlets – the street fighting, contemptuous words and gestures, eyes full of fear or hatred. As outsiders, Margaret and I noticed and felt the need to explain many things which locals had grown up with and took for granted. I thought that history must hold the answer even before I began my long program of research in libraries and archives. It seemed that there must have been a larger violence, a more comprehensive terror in the past, in order to make sense of the present. European settlement in North Queensland was barely one hundred years old. Townsville celebrated its centenary a month or two before we arrived. North Queenslanders were still attached to the frontier era – that time of pioneer settlement, frontal assault on indigenous society and bloody expropriation of land. Avenues of understanding opened up for me when I heard the stories of Aboriginal and Islander families and as I began to read the written documents left by pastoralists, sugar planters, officials and travellers.

Indigenous people had their own informal, oral, dissident history of European settlement. There could have been few families without their personal stories of violence and suffering, of great wrongs done to their own kin. Memories of the killing times were fresh, and still called up powerful emotions. One story was told by a family who were descended from an East European settler who married an Aboriginal woman from the rainforest. A second continental migrant in the district followed suit. On the eve of his marriage he came to visit the family's house, bringing his Colt revolver with him. He handed it over to his friend, saying that because he had killed so many Aborigines with it he never wanted to see it again.

A very old lady recalled a childhood memory when members of her clan had been shot for stealing sugar cane. An even more compelling story about a Native Police raid in the rainforest north of Townsville was recorded by one of my research assistants:

> Big mob come up from Atherton
> all the native police come up
> all got the rifle, all got handcuffs
> fire for bullock, roast im, altogether
> bullock is for tucker
> shoot im altogether, shoot im altogether
> chuck im in the fire
> all the revolvers going on
> talk about smell
> nobody gonna be alive

chuck im in the fire, half alive,
sing out
you all finished no more
Native police shot im all
Widow come back cryin
she lose im husband
all finished, they shotem live
all crying come home
to this valley here

I realised from my reading that Aborigines told similar stories in other parts of Australia. The anthropologists Ronald and
Catherine Berndt reported in 1951 that frontier conflict was
still 'vividly remembered' in Arnhem Land. In northern New
South Wales their colleague Marie Reay found in the 1940s that
'punitive expeditions and other massacres of Aborigines occupy
an important place in the history of the mixed blood groups as
interpreted by themselves'. The site of the nearest massacre was
'always known' and was seen as an important landmark. Many
accounts of violence were subsequently recorded by researchers
in the 1970s and 1980s. My experience was that Aboriginal
families were surprised that migloos were interested in their
stories, and even more surprised when they realised that they
were writing a new sort of whitefella history. I was told on a
number of occasions by old murris that they never thought they
would ever hear a migloo talking or writing in the way that I did.

But as powerful and moving as Aboriginal stories were, the
main research effort had to be with the European records. They
carried the authority of the written word; they were put down at
a set time and in a specific place. What is more, there were a great

many of them. In the early 1970s Noel Loos completed a PhD thesis on the history of contact and conflict in North Queensland. At the same time I received a major research grant to work on Queensland as a whole but started with the settlement of the south and central parts of the colony. I published an article entitled 'Violence, the Aboriginals and the Australian Historian' in the literary journal *Meanjin* in December 1972, and in August 1973 delivered a paper on frontier violence in Queensland to the history section of the Australian and New Zealand Association for the Advancement of Science Congress in Perth. By then Noel and I had uncovered a vast amount of material about pioneer settlement. We knew that violence was ubiquitous, that it overwhelmed every other possible aspect of the story. The evidence for this was abundant, various and incontrovertible. No article, no single book, could do justice to the great volume of evidence that came pouring out of the official government records, the newspapers, the travellers' tales, the reminiscences. There was far more there than I ever imagined when I began my research into Aboriginal–European relations. There was far more than any of the traditional histories of Australia had suggested.

Finding the evidence was one thing; writing it up and presenting it to the public was quite another, particularly as it would obviously be controversial and challenging and likely to attract a hostile response from many people brought up on the conventional story of peaceful settlement and heroic pioneers. The weight of evidence had totally convinced me that the history of exploration, of land settlement, of the squatting movement and the pastoral industry and much else had to be rewritten. But neither Noel Loos nor I spoke with much authority. Our hard-won evidence was all we had to carry our cause.

We decided to compile registers of the number of Europeans — and other immigrants such as Chinese and Melanesians — who had been killed by the Aborigines in the course of frontier conflict between the 1840s and the 1890s. Here was something that could be counted with at least a measure of confidence. We combed official records, inquest files and newspapers, and by the time I delivered my paper in Perth we had reached at least tentative conclusions. We estimated that there were about 400 deaths in my area during the thirty years from 1841, when pastoral expansion was just beginning, to the early 1870s, and somewhere between 420 and 440 in North Queensland between the first settlement at Bowen in 1861 and the passage of the Aborigines Protection Act in 1897. We concluded that there had been between 800 and 850 deaths in the fifty-odd years it took the Europeans to occupy the most productive parts of the colony. Many others were wounded, but their numbers were never recorded. It may have been as many as 1000 or more. There were perhaps as many as 2000 European casualties in Queensland's 'border wars'.

The number of deaths fluctuated considerably from year to year, from as low as one or two to as high as thirty or forty. Peaks of between twenty-five and thirty were reached in the years of rapid pastoral expansion, like the early 1840s, which saw the occupation of the Darling Downs and Brisbane Valley; the late 1840s and early 1850s, when squatters pushed into the Wide Bay and Burnett districts; and in the early 1860s, when frontages were taken up all along the rivers of the Fitzroy Basin. In some new pastoral districts up to 10 or 20 per cent of the initial workforce may have died as a result of Aboriginal attack. As pastoral expansion slowed the death rate fell, but it shot up again with the North Queensland gold rushes of the 1870s to reach an all-time peak of forty-six in 1874. Though violent deaths rarely exceeded two or three a month, frontier conflict was an inescapable accompaniment of Queensland life for fifty years.

The attitudes of the settlers could not be quantified. But they provided an abundance of remarkably frank observations about frontier conflict, about the Aborigines and about indiscriminate killing. The brutality and callousness of many statements was both surprising and shocking. Once again it was a voice that had been filtered out of mainstream historical writing. From the perspective of today's values the settlers condemned themselves out of their own mouths. The growing brutality of colonial society was watched with alarm by more tender-minded contemporaries. One wrote to the *Moreton Bay Free Press* on 15 September 1859, just before Queensland was separated from New South Wales, deeply concerned that an 'abominable feeling' was becoming a principle in the minds of the men of Queensland. They were coming to believe that it was not murder to kill an Aborigine in cold blood and that any white man was 'justified in taking the law into his own hands'. A similar letter appeared in the *Rockhampton Bulletin* on 25 June 1867 about 'The Recent Outrages on the Blacks', in which the writer expressed alarm that news about atrocities on the Aborigines was so easily accepted. He feared the whole community was being brutalised:

> Already the evil leaven has begun to work. I have frequently
> felt grieved and indignant at the levity with which many of
> the colonial youth speak of those outrages on the blacks.

When reading comments like these, I sensed that the concern being shown marked the emergence of traditions of brutality that were still discernible in North Queensland one hundred years later.

Records produced many accounts of raids by the Native Police which mirrored the rainforest story collected by my research assistant. There were graphic descriptions of the infamous raid by Lieutenant Bligh and his troopers in Maryborough in 1860, when the town blacks were gunned down in full view of the townspeople; one young man was shot in the back while trying to swim across the river. Another account of atrocity appeared in the *Rockhampton Bulletin* on 18 June 1867 in a letter from a resident of a small nearby mining community. People woke at dawn to the sound of gunfire:

> The first surmise was that it was some early kangaroo hunter, but the crack was too sharp for that, and the number of discharges too numerous to allow of such a supposition bearing a second thought, and a rush in the direction of the camp was immediately made by those who were so early a-foot, where a scene presented itself alike brutal on the part of the perpetrators, and revolting to the feelings of those who saw it. The native camp was deserted, but around the fires nearest to the township lay the scanty garments of men, gins and piccaninnies, many of them saturated with blood, while the track of the fugitives could be easily traced by the trail of blood leading from the fires in every direction. At the fire nearest the Creek, which separates the camp from the township, and around which a number of blacks apparently had been sleeping, two pools of blood and brains showed where foul murder had been perpetrated, and a gin's clothing, all stained with blood, was also found,

exactly as if the unfortunate black had just left the articles on finding herself wounded. A little further on, close to the fire, where one person, probably an old man, had passed the night, another puddle of blood and brains was found, the surrounding ground bore all the traces of the flight of wounded men, and of dead bleeding bodies having been dragged over it.

There were many such graphic accounts of atrocity in colonial Queensland's many newspapers. They were confronting and shocking. It was not just that such awful events took place but that they were so openly discussed and described with unblinking candour, and it was unusual for anything to happen as a result of the publication of such accounts. Comment from the government was rarely forthcoming, enquiries were infrequent, prosecution almost unheard-of. And not all reporting of atrocity was as disapproving as that of the *Rockhampton Bulletin*'s correspondent. Many accounts made light of shooting Aborigines, or at least justified such actions as being part of the brutal necessities of pioneering. In an article entitled 'Taming the Niggers', published in the *Townsville Herald* on 2 February 1907, an old pioneer, using the nom de plume 'H7H', boasted of his part in a punitive expedition:

It was estimated that over 150 myalls 'bit the dust' that morning, and unfortunately many women and children shared the same fate. In that wild, yelling, rushing mob it was hard to avoid shooting the women and babies, and there were men in that mob of whites who would ruthlessly destroy anything possessing a black hide.

The writer went on to give an account of a second raid on a camp, following the death by spearing of a station owner. The party of Europeans crept up towards the sleeping camp, where the presumed killers of the white man were thought to be:

> They slept soundly those myalls after their long march, and could have had no thought of us being so close to them, for we were within revolver shot of them before our presence was discovered, and then it was too late, for muddled with sleep, sore-footed, weary, and panic stricken they offered no resistance, and many of them were 'wiped out' before they could gain their feet. Talk of the 'Furies of Hell', that night's work amongst those myalls with the white man's rifle and tomahawk would make 'Hell's Furies' blush. How those gins and kiddies shrieked when we got amongst them. The blood of the white man was up and nothing with a black hide escaped death that night . . . for when we had finished our work and drawn off, and in daylight came to view the white man's work of vengeance bucks, gins and piccaninnies were lying dead in all directions, and not a thing in camp moved or breathed.

The writer concluded his article with an apology, an explanation of why he and his fellow frontiersmen had engaged in massacre:

> The foregoing will serve in some way to give an idea of the manner in which the myalls were originally tamed and taught to obey the law of the white man. It may appear cold blooded murder to some to wipe out a whole camp for killing, perhaps a couple of bullocks, but then each member of the tribe

must be held equally guilty, and therefore, it would be impossible to discriminate. I do not wish to make out that the pioneer white men of this north land were in any way heroes, although they to a certain extent needed pluck to face such odds as they were pitted against in these myalls, although the niggers were only armed with spears . . . The writer never held a man guilty of murder who wiped out a nigger. They should be classed with the black snake and death adder, and treated accordingly.

This article was apparently written about events that had occurred some years before. There may have been an element of exaggeration and bravado in it. But I don't think that anyone who has researched frontier history would doubt its general authenticity or that such raids on Aboriginal camps were commonplace. Reading it again now, many years after I first discovered it, I am still shocked by the events described, the sentiments expressed, the justifications propounded. It is important, therefore, to place the article in context. It was printed in the daily paper of a major provincial city in 1907, six years after Federation. The writer confessed to mass murder without the slightest concern about prosecution or even of social opprobrium. As another correspondent, 'Amicus Nigorum', asked on 14 February: 'Are we living in the enlightened twentieth century and allowing this to go on?' And what, he enquired, were the government and its officials doing? The evidence was surely sufficient to set the machinery of law in motion. If not, then justice must 'indeed be blind, as well as blindfolded'.

But how much did contemporaries know about brutal events out on the far frontiers of settlement? We can never know for certain, but many articles and letters relating to punitive expeditions and massacres appeared in the metropolitan newspapers. The Queensland government certainly knew what was happening. The official records include many complaints about frontier violence. They were answered with brief dismissive letters or not answered at all. Histories written in the nineteenth century were far franker about frontier conflict than those published in the twentieth century. The three-volume *History of Australia* by G.W. Rusden, published in 1883, was particularly scathing about the treatment of the Aborigines in Queensland. Having dealt in detail with atrocities committed and condoned, Rusden declared: 'How does the heart ache, to think of the Aborigines done to death and left mangled and stark on the soil of Queensland'.

My detailed research, which initially focused on Queensland, broadened out eventually to deal with the whole of Australia. While I was working in libraries and archives all over the country and in Britain, many other scholars produced studies of contact and conflict in various parts of the continent. By the early 1980s it was possible to draw some conclusions about the continent as a whole. It appeared that conflict was practically universal around the fringes of settlement, although there were important regional differences which resulted from the period of first contact, the varying policies of government, the prior knowledge of Europeans possessed by Aborigines, particular geographic and climatic conditions, the density of European settlement and the nature of the settlers' economic activity. I found myself agreeing with the nineteenth-century writers who had attempted to arrive at an overview of the process of colonisation. In 1880, for instance, the ethnographers L. Fison and A.W. Howitt declared in their book *Kamilaroi and Kurnai*:

It may be stated broadly that the advance of settlement has, upon the frontier at least, been marked by a line of blood. The actual conflict of the two races has varied in intensity and in duration, as the various native tribes have themselves in mental and physical character . . . But the tide of settlement has advanced along an ever widening line, breaking the tribes with its first wave and overwhelming their wrecks with its flood.

The Victorian ethnographer Edward Curr reached a similar conclusion a few years later, writing in his book *The Australian Race* in 1886:

In the first place the meeting of the Aboriginal tribes of Australia and the White pioneer results as a rule in war which lasts from six months to ten years, according to the nature of the country, the amount of settlement which takes place in the neighbourhood, and the proclivities of the individuals concerned. When several squatters settle in proximity, and the country they occupy is easy of access and without fastnesses to which the Blacks can retreat, the period of warfare is usually short and the bloodshed not excessive. On the other hand, in districts which are not easily traversed on horseback in which the Whites are few in number and food is procurable by the Blacks in fastnesses, the term is usually prolonged and the slaughter more considerable.

What Fison, Howitt and Curr appreciated was that the process of settlement, violence and dispossession unfolded over a long period of time across the vast land mass. It was an under-standing about the continuity of conflict that virtually disap-peared from the history books during the first two-thirds of the twentieth century. Conflict which started on the outskirts of the settlement on Sydney Cove within a few months of the arrival of the First Fleet continued to occur sporadically for the next 140 years. This was, perhaps, not unexpected given the size of Aus-tralia, the lack of effective policing in remote areas and the widely scattered nature of the settler population in many regions. Small-scale private feuds and vendettas were probably inevitable on largely lawless frontiers. But what requires much more explanation was the persistent involvement of govern-ments in punitive expeditions against people who were not ene-mies but British subjects.

In December 1790, Governor Phillip sent a detachment of fifty marines to punish the clans living around the northern shore of Botany Bay for spearing his servant. The troops were instructed to capture six men or to shoot and decapitate them if that could not be effected. The punishment was to be indiscriminate, dispro-portionate and almost certainly illegal. Phillip had decided that he would 'strike a decisive blow' against the offending clans in order to convince them of British superiority and to 'infuse an universal terror' which he hoped would 'prevent further mischief'. In August 1928 one white man was speared in central Australia and another was wounded by Walpiri tribesmen. A police party rode out and killed as many as seventy men, women and children in revenge. A subsequent Federal Government enquiry exonerated the members of the police party. The two punitive expeditions were 138 years apart. But both were official government opera-tions which set out to wreak revenge for the murder of one white man. Both were concerned with creating a 'universal terror'. We will never know how many official punitive expeditions – conducted by the military or the police – set forth to punish the blacks between 1790 and 1928. But there must have been many. Throughout the nineteenth century there would have been at least a handful of expeditions every single year. As far as I know, no white soldier or policeman ever faced trial over actions taken as part of a punitive expedition.

The line of blood runs from 1790 to 1928, joining up all the disparate punitive expeditions, although they must have varied widely in effectiveness, duration, personnel and tactics. All were premised on the assumption that it was both necessary and legitimate to kill Aboriginal men, women and children without summons, trial or conviction, although parties often spuriously justified their actions by claiming they were merely trying to arrest offenders for whom warrants had been issued. The killing was always indiscriminate. The most fanciful and flimsy evidence was often used to identify those individuals deemed guilty of offences. It was universally thought sufficient to identify the right 'mob' and to punish all and sundry, to assume collective guilt. Most expeditions were motivated by the desire for revenge because of attacks on settlers or more often on their property. The revenge was almost always disproportionate. It was never a case of an eye for an eye or a tooth for a tooth. There was almost universally a desire to raise the stakes – to use far more violence in return for whatever the Aborigines had done or were thought to have done. There was a constant refrain of the need to teach the blacks a lesson, to show them once and for all that resistance was both dangerous and futile, that acquiescence was the only answer.

Having counted the number of settlers killed by the Aborigines in Queensland I decided that I should try to estimate the death rate on both sides of the frontier during Australia's many years of intermittent frontier conflict. I first published my estimates in *The Other Side of the Frontier* in 1981. By then a number of regional studies had provided additional local information to add to our Queensland figures. I explained:

> There is now enough regional accounting to make an intelligent guess about the country as a whole. It seems reasonable to suggest that Aborigines killed somewhere between 2000 and 2500 Europeans in the course of the invasion and settlement of the continent. There were many hundreds of others who were injured and carried both physical and psychological scars for the rest of their lives.

But how many Aborigines died in frontier conflict? That was a much more difficult problem to unravel. There were some nineteenth-century estimates of local death tolls by missionaries, protectors and settlers. But over much of the continent the bodies were more likely to be incinerated rather than enumerated, to use the memorable phrase of Queensland historian Ray Evans. A number of regional studies published during the 1970s provided useful information. But even when all the available data had been collected there were still far too many imponderables to allow anything more than a poorly informed guess. I thought it probable that at least 20 000 Aborigines were killed as a direct result of conflict with the settlers. If anything, it was an estimate that erred on the side of caution. The death toll may have been significantly higher. But even 20 000 was a figure of enormous consequence. It was far higher than I would have thought probable when I began my research and certainly higher than a reader would deduce from most twentieth-century history books. What was also significant was that as far as I could see no-one had ever bothered to try and quantify the Aboriginal death toll. At the time I was thinking about these problems I often asked myself the obvious questions – Why didn't I know? Why wasn't I ever told during all the years of my education? Perhaps historians had simply been uninterested in such questions. Or was it a matter of conscious and deliberate avoidance, of a desire to cover up the less appealing parts in the nation's story?

That case had been persuasively argued, as noted above, by Professor W.E.H. Stanner in his Boyer lectures in 1968, and by Professor C.D. Rowley two years later in his book *The Destruction of Aboriginal Society*. There was a 'mental block' which prevented Australians from coming to terms with the past. The general view was 'What is done is done and should now be forgotten'. There was a strong community sentiment that raking up the misdeeds of the past would serve no useful purpose and this was reflected in the way history was taught in schools. Textbooks had been bowdlerised to exclude the less attractive aspects of the process of land settlement.

I found plenty of evidence to support Rowley's and Stanner's arguments. In the late nineteenth century many writers quite consciously avoided references to the nature and extent of frontier conflict. They said things like 'it is well to draw a veil over the dark side of the picture' or 'there one would willingly draw a veil over the sad picture'. This was the view of the eminent ethnographers Baldwin Spencer and F.J. Gillen. In their book of 1912, *Across Australia*, they observed that there were parts of the country where it was necessary 'to draw the veil over the past history of the relationship between the blackfellow and the white man'.

Evasion and reticence about racial violence was apparent in more recent works. In 1960 the distinguished surgeon and ethnographer J.B. Cleland complained that it was a 'matter of deep regret that atrocities committed by unscrupulous white people on our natives years ago are raked up and recounted for propaganda purposes'. In her *History of Australia* of 1963 Marjorie Barnard agreed that little was to be gained by 'recounting all the recorded black and white incidents'. The leading politician and scholar Paul Hasluck displayed a similar sensitivity to past violence, a fastidiousness that verged on self-censorship. In his 1942 book *Black Australians:A Survey of Native Policy in Western Australia 1829–1897,* he announced in the first few pages that, when it came to accounts of violence, 'easy sensationalism' would be 'scrupulously avoided'. He promised his reader that in the 'scant references to violence, no more will be quoted than seems necessary to show the measures taken or the attitude of colonists . . .' Later in the book Hasluck allowed himself to deal with two incidents when significant numbers of Aborigines were shot – the Battle of Pinjarra on the Murray River in 1834 and the so-called La Grange Bay affair of 1864. But he explained that the two cases had been cited 'not for sensationalism nor with any wish to give them undue prominence in the story of violence'.

I was appalled at such reticence, which appeared to lead to a wilful avoidance of important aspects of Australian history. In my 1972 article in *Meanjin* I argued that, in writing the Aborigines out of the story, historians had also 'written out much of the violence, thereby seriously distorting our view of the past'. As I researched more widely and sensed the scale, intensity and impact of frontier violence, I took the view that conventional historical accounts not only distorted the past but were also guilty of perpetrating grave injustices on indigenous Australians, who were not treated with the seriousness and gravity that was due to them. In the conclusion to *The Other Side of the Frontier,* I declared with self-righteous vehemence:

> Frontier violence was political violence. We cannot ignore it because it took place on the fringes of European settlement. Twenty thousand blacks were killed before federation. Their burial mound stands out as a landmark of awesome size on the peaceful plains of colonial history. If the bodies had been white our histories would be heavy with their story, a forest of monuments would celebrate their sacrifice. The much noted actions of rebel colonists are trifling in comparison. The Kellys and their kind, even Eureka diggers and Vinegar Hill convicts, are diminished when measured against the hundreds of clans who fought frontier settlers for well over a century. In parts of the continent the Aboriginal death toll overshadows even that of the overseas wars of the twentieth century. About 5,000 Europeans from Australia north of the Tropic of Capricorn died in the five wars between the outbreak of the Boer War and the end of the Vietnam engagement. But in a similar period – say the seventy years between the first settlement in north Queensland in 1861 and the early 1930s – as many as 10,000 blacks were killed in skirmishes with the Europeans in north Australia.

IX

The Killing Times

In an article in the journal *Eureka Street* of October 1998, Peter Cochrane suggested that it was now a throwaway line in Australian history circles that in my writing I overdo the 'violence theme'. Similar comments have been made to me many times during the last twenty years – at public meetings, from talkback radio callers, in personal letters and in newspaper articles. It is my writing about frontier conflict that is most in contention and which most readily attracts the label of black-armband history. Many people believe I present a negative and destructive view of the past, which undermines national self-confidence and creates a marked sense of guilt. Anonymous letter-writers declare that I am a traitor to Australia or to the white race, or to both. Others accuse me of deliberately stirring up trouble, provoking discontent, reviving old hatreds. One recent anonymous letter was addressed:

Henry Reynolds
Ratbag fellow
James Cook University

It read:

Sir,

You are nothing but a shit stirring academic. Keep it up and you, and the likes of you, will probably be the first victims of the strife you are hell bent on creating

What makes the likes of you?

Is it the rarefied air of the university?

Is it the company you keep?

Is it because you feel you are endowed with a superior view of the world?

There is no doubt in the minds of many of the 'common' folk that James Cook in Townsville is a hotbed of weirdos who think they are going to save the world.

P.S. You'll never believe it but I've got nothing to do with politics. I just think you're a trouble maker.

The attack was personal, but the problem here is a general one. In the past anyone who spoke out about violence was regarded as a stirrer, an irresponsible troublemaker. That was no doubt why Paul Hasluck was so extraordinarily careful when dealing with the subject. But the records are there in the libraries and archives. They overflow with evidence of violence. The message they carry is incontrovertible. To hide the violence it is necessary to hide the history. What I found most surprising in the records of colonial Australia was the frank and open discussion of racial violence and the public acceptance of violence which that discussion signalled. The newspapers were the most revealing and most copious source of material. This was particularly true of Queensland, which had many small provincial newspapers which began publication when violence still haunted local hinterlands. There was little reticence or fastidiousness in discussion about how to 'deal with the blacks', although there was always debate and disagreement. There were invariably citizens who counselled clemency. But there were also journalists and correspondents from the frontier who spoke openly of their own brutal deeds, who boasted of deadly prowess or of involvement in massacres, or who advocated atrocity from the comfort of editorial desks. After several shepherds had been speared in the district in 1867, the editor of the Clermont paper the *Peak Downs Telegram* argued that 'a war of extermination is the only policy to pursue, the alternative being an abandonment of the country which no sane man will advocate for an instant'. Letter-writers openly urged atrocity: a correspondent from North Queensland wrote to the Brisbane weekly the *Queenslander* in 1876 that 'our best shots are after them; I am off too; there will be weeping and wailing some-where shortly after I have started, you bet'.

In the course of my research I read over fifty colonial news-papers – covering many years in some cases. I read every frontier newspaper that had survived, wherever it was or whatever its condition – in the basement of city libraries, in rural council chambers and newspaper offices. A few had been microfilmed but many were in 'hard copy'. With some files you had the impression they hadn't been opened for a hundred years. A few papers were still folded in the way in which they left the news-paper offices all those years before.

I was often shocked by what I read. The papers told a story about the country profoundly different from the one I had grown up with. I felt many things – pity for the Aborigines, anger at the way they were dealt with and with the profound injustice of it all. But I was also disillusioned and disappointed because things had been so much worse, more violent, more openly brutal than I had imagined when I began my research. There I was, a lecturer in Australian history, with a masters degree in the subject, and yet I had no idea about what had gone on all around the frontiers of Australia for well over a century. And the continuity was remarkable. There were, of course, differences in language, style and emphasis. But the sorts of things which were being said in Hobart's newspapers in the 1820s and Sydney's in the 1830s were reiterated in Queensland in the 1880s, Western Australia in the 1890s and the Northern Territory in the 1920s. Once the frontier receded, there was time and space for reflection and balance and compassion. But every part of Australia had its season of sudden death and brutal dispossession. There were few, if any, pockets of peace, despite special pleading for one part of Australia or another.

The more I read about frontier conflict, the more certain I became that the central problem had been there from the beginning. It was always at the heart of things. The settlers came to acquire the land which was already owned and occupied and had been so for many thousands of years. The British decided they would take the land without a treaty, without negotiation, and without any attempt to purchase it. Whenever and wherever the indigenous landowners resisted the European incursion or attempted to impose their law on the newcomers, the only answer was force. It is hard to see how it could have been otherwise. The result was predetermined. The Europeans would get all the land they wanted, but to effect the expropriation they would have to kill some of the Aborigines and terrorise the others into acquiescence. This recipe for successful colonisation was well understood by the early governors. They expressed almost the same idea quite independently in different colonies. As we have already seen, Governor Phillip decided in 1790 to 'infuse an universal terror . . . to prevent further mischief'. In 1816 his successor, Governor Macquarie, planned to attack the tribes on the outskirts of the settlement 'so as to Strike them with Terror against Committing Similar acts of violence in the future'. Twelve years later, in Tasmania, Governor Arthur's Executive Council declared martial law, the purpose of which was 'To inspire them with terror . . .' which would be 'the only effectual means of security for the future'. In 1834 Western Australia's military commandant, F.C. Irwin, believed it necessary to subject the Aborigines to 'some severe defeat' to convince them of European superiority and to put a stop to the 'petty and harassing warfare'. In their own way countless frontier settlers followed suit. They regarded their attacks on Aboriginal camps as exemplary violence. It was done to teach the blacks a lesson they would never forget, to enforce submission and subordination.

What governors and vengeful settlers realised was that a little bit of violence goes a long way. It could be used to terrorise whole territories. Its impact spread geographically. The news of atrocity carried the message of atrocity. The white men wielded superior force and had the will to use it. The impact of such atrocity endured: the lessons were learnt and were passed on to children and grandchildren. Aboriginal oral tradition taught that it was dangerous to backchat a white man. The stories both inspired resistance and counselled caution and the need for a show of subordination.

The lessons were constantly reinforced. Confederate white communities agreed about the need to keep the blacks in their place, to watch with the harsh clear eye of the eagle for any sign of insubordination. This was as true of New South Wales in the 1820s as it was of more remote areas in the late nineteenth century and early twentieth century. A humanitarian-minded visitor to Sydney and its hinterland in the 1820s observed that the Aborigines were in a state of exposure to caprices and wanton punishment. 'The White', he declared, 'assumes within himself the power of punishment, and inflicts it upon the black just as the feeling of the moment impels'. Forty years later, in Brisbane, a correspondent to the local newspaper remarked how private individuals took it on themselves to 'administer a sound thrashing for offences against the decency or peace of the neighbourhood'. In 1884 a writer in the *Queenslander* noted that 'every man seems to consider himself as quite justified in carrying out the utmost vigour of the law towards an Aboriginal, often for some very trivial and insignificant crime'.

The terrible truth was that in those frontier areas where white and black lived side by side, European men virtually had power of life and death over Aborigines. This was so in the more remote parts of Australia until the 1930s. Anyone could kill an Aboriginal man or rape an Aboriginal woman with little chance of ever being brought before a court. Social disapproval might follow, but it would rarely be universal. The Queensland official Archibald Meston toured the south-west of the colony just before the turn of the century. He found the station workers living under 'extraordinary terrorism', although many of them were 'fine athletic fellows'. The reason for their subjugation was that they were 'scared into a belief that their employers wielded the power of life and death'. Charles Rowley observed in 1970 that 'There are still persons living who could kill an Aboriginal with impunity if not legality when they were young; and Aboriginal tribesmen who remember such incidents'.

As I read such material I thought as much about the present as the past. It had such resonance, such power of explanation. I understood the reason for the downcast eyes, the fear of challenging a migloo even with too confident a glance, gesture or gait. This was why I had seen such fear in the eyes of Aborigines I met and such caution in the way they weighed up and watched migloos before they dropped their mask, spoke their minds or confided their feelings. It was such constant reminders, the ever-present echoes of past violence, that continued to spur me on in my task of researching the story of the frontier. It was no idle search for sensation.

I knew from the start the work would be controversial. In the fraught atmosphere of North Queensland in the 1960s and 1970s, I was only too well aware that new historical interpretation would be extremely provocative, that along with many other changes going on it would be seen as challenging to a way of life, to old assumptions, to a hierarchy of status, all of which had been in place since the early years of settlement. Had I spoken out about these things in pubs and clubs around the north, rather than writing earnestly of them in academic journals and serious books, I would have ended up on my back many times over. I also knew that it would be profoundly irresponsible to sensationalise the many terrible stories I was unearthing. They were shocking partly because they had been so well buried, so

effectively forgotten. And few people living in communities like
Townsville would deliberately court a rise in racial tension. It was
all too close to the bone. So history of violence was never just an
academic or a scholarly question for me. I could never completely separate in my mind past and present, thought and action,
word and deed. It was also obvious to me at a very early stage in
my research that what I was doing was inescapably political. It
was work which, of necessity, engaged the world.

I started with the assumption that my writing would attract
both criticism and scepticism. Hence it was important to be
cautious about evidence, to check it carefully and to discount
material that seemed unreliable or that related to events that
appeared improbable. I think I erred on the side of scepticism
when it came to accepting accounts of massacres or of the mass
poisoning of Aborigines. My estimate that 20 000 Aborigines
were killed on the frontier of settlement was a cautious one. It is
much more likely to have understated the true figures. I felt the
need to try to exhaust all possible sources and to add incident
upon incident, example upon example, before I was confident
about making generalisations. The publication in the 1970s and
1980s of work by other scholars working on similar evidence
strengthened my conviction that my interpretation was on the
right track, as did the gradual expansion of my own research outward from Queensland to cover the whole of Australia. But it
was only after ten years' work that I felt confident enough to
attempt to present a synthesis of my research, which appeared in
The Other Side of the Frontier in 1981.

Do I make too much of violence? Given my years of research,
do I have a vested interest in the subject? Has it been a meal
ticket? Was it a means of attracting attention to an obscure

career? These are not easy questions to answer. What possible measure can be applied? How much is too much?

One way of responding is to ask the question of how historians would handle the subject if 20 000 Europeans had been killed within Australia in domestic conflict or civil war. In the first place, it is clear that such conflict would not have disappeared from the history books and school curricula in the way that the 'border wars' did. The events leading to such conflict would have been debated many times over and partisan schools of interpreters would have arisen. Many Australians would presumably see the fallen as martyrs to one cause or another. Songs, poetry, painting would celebrate their sacrifice. Days of remembrance would have been declared, monuments raised in the martyrs' memory. I'm not sure that many voices would emerge to declare that the country was making too much of violence if the bodies had been white and they had died in causes articulated in English. European violence would be seen as political violence – as a serious matter of competing principles, ideologies and moralities. But the suggestion that too much is made of frontier violence carries a hidden freight – the implication that it was rather a simple and mindless matter lacking high principle and moral gravity. Even those who generally sympathise with the Aborigines err on this account. The trouble, they suggest, can be explained in simple terms as the result of violent, racist behaviour by European men – characteristics they took with them to the frontier. It is often suggested that Aborigines were shot and hunted for sport. But such interpretations diminish the conflict, seeing it as criminal or sadistic rather than political and strategic – the instrument for the acquisition of a whole continent.

Few Aborigines believe white historians spend too much

time dealing with violence. They say so again and again in speeches, in their writing and in conversation. I have heard the same judgement delivered many times over the years. They think the new interest is long overdue and harmonises with their own oral tradition. They feel that at last white Australia has admitted things they have always known; that finally the truth is being told. And telling the truth is central to the Aboriginal agenda for reconciliation. They want to have the truth told about numerous things – about the taking of the children, about the exploitation of labour, the systematic abuse of women. But above all is the matter of violence, the long history of frontier conflict. They want white Australia to own, to accept, to identify with a past that they know only too well. Reconciliation means the reconciling of the two stories about what happened when pioneer settlers met indigenous people all around a vast, moving, ragged frontier. They want us to talk about the line of blood. They want us to take it seriously and treat it with gravity, to recognise that violence was not just an aberration or an accident but rather that it was central to the creation of modern Australia. They would like us to admit that settlement grew out of the barrel of a gun. For how else can their loss of ancestral lands be understood and explained?

Acceptance of new stories about the frontier will inevitably replace or significantly change old ones in ways that may not, at first, be obvious. In my case, the history I was researching and writing dramatically and permanently altered my view of the so-called 'noble frontiersman'. Like other people of my generation, I grew up with a wholly positive and romantic view of the outback and of the bushman. That was perhaps easier in Tasmania than in parts of Australia where people had first-hand experience of 'the bush' and knew what it was really like. Our education portrayed Australian history as a saga of exploration and pioneering – a long, hard but largely successful story of settling the new land. And the land itself had been the enemy, not the Aborigines. So the struggle was peaceful, heroic and wholly admirable. These ideas had come to me from many sources – books, magazines, films, radio programs. Our primary-school reading books contained Henry Lawson stories and poems by 'Banjo' Paterson and other versifiers of the *Bulletin* school. And how we loved reading the rhythmic, demotic and laconic lines of 'The Sick Stockrider' and 'Clancy of the Overflow'. They were so much more interesting than the English Romantic poems that accompanied them in the readers. And they were much easier to understand. 'Hold hard Ned, and lift me down once more' or 'There was movement at the Station/For the word had got around' beat 'Hail to thee, blithe spirit!/Bird thou never wert' hands down.

Like many other Australians of my age, I'm sure I grew up believing that the bush was the source of the nation's distinctive attitudes and values. When I gradually developed political views, they emerged coloured with the mystique of the outback. The egalitarianism I treasured I attributed to the bush worker rather than to my own social environment in Hobart or to home-grown political traditions. The thesis I wrote in my honours year was an enthusiastic – and rather breathless – celebration of outback egalitarianism and the benign and creative influence of the inland environment. I quoted with much approval the English journalist Francis Adams's assertion that:

> the gulf between colony and colony is transversable compared to that great frontier that exists between the people of

the Slope and the Interior . . . where the Marine rainfall
flags out and is lost, a new climate, and, in a certain sense,
a new race begins to unfold itself . . . it is not one hundred,
but three and five hundred miles that you must go back from
the sea if you would find yourself face to face with the one
powerful and unique national type yet produced in the
new land.

It was among the bush workers, I agreed, that distinctive Australian values like egalitarianism and mateship developed. And in
the literature of the *Bulletin* school those values were dissemi-
nated to a larger, urban audience. Joseph Furphy's *Such is Life* was
a favourite source of quotations. 'Human equality', Furphy
asserted to my delight, 'was self evident as human variety, and
impregnable as any mathematical axiom'. I was, if anything, even
more pleased with his celebration of bush virtues in the well-
known passage:

without doubt, it is easier to acquire gentlemanly deport-
ment than axe-man's muscles; easier to criticise an opera
than to identify a beast seen casually twelve months before;
easier to dress becomingly than to make a bee-line, straight as
the sighting of a theodolite, across strange country in foggy
weather; easier to recognise the various costly vintages than
to live contentedly on the smell of an oily rag.

I was deeply influenced by Russel Ward's book *The Australian
Legend*, which I read while I was writing my honours thesis. It
synthesised many of the ideas with which I was engaged. I fully
accepted his basic thesis about the origins of the distinctive

Australian character – the laconic, egalitarian, anti-authoritarian, resourceful bloke. Ward argued that these characteristics emerged early in the colonial period from among three distinct groups – the convicts, the Irish and the native born. These groups were heavily over-represented among the 'nomad tribe' of bush workers in the outback, where a unique environment and political economy fostered the emergence of characteristics which by the 1890s were recognised as being distinctively Australian.

I began to question Ward's ideas while I was working on Tasmanian history because it didn't seem to have much relevance to island experience. But it was the vast amount of material about actual conditions on the frontier that made much of the legend untenable. It was as if Russel and I had researched totally different places or had worked on quite distinctive periods of time, such disparate things did we see. The implications of the new history of the frontier that I was helping to write only slowly dawned on me. I did not give up my romantic notions about the outback easily or willingly. But the evidence pushed me inch by inch towards a quite different story from the one I had grown up with and celebrated in my first serious work of research.

The main problem with Ward's account of life 'up the Country' was that it was an outback almost, but not completely, devoid of Aborigines. He suggests that the 'typically Australian' characteristics had already developed by 1850 in the pastoral regions of south-eastern Australia. But the white population up country was necessarily small and scattered on hundreds of pastoral stations. In many areas Aborigines outnumbered Europeans, although the population was rapidly declining. Many stockmen and shepherds cohabited with Aboriginal women for longer or shorter periods or raped them when the occasion presented itself. Members of the nomad tribe were in the forefront of the border wars. They manned the punitive expeditions, large and small. Many of them shot Aborigines and in turn they lived in fear of a spear in the back and knew of fellow workers who had been bludgeoned to death. Those who shrank from the brutal business of the punitive expedition were often forced to participate and thereby made to share the responsibility and culpability. Even if some stockmen avoided direct involvement, they certainly knew all about what was going on and showed their complicity by refusing to divulge any information to the authorities. Magistrates and other officials usually found it impossible to crack the code of silence and the close confederation of the nomad tribe to gain evidence about atrocities.

The greatest problem I had with Ward's account of life up the country was its avoidance of the pervasive violence. But it was not just a case of serious omission. He went much further than that, suggesting that Australia had a uniquely peaceful history because of the 'mild' Aborigines, whose reaction to settler hostility was 'so sporadic and ineffectual that men seldom had to go armed on the Australian frontier'. How could he have missed the guns? They were ubiquitous; an essential adjunct to life in the bush. Evidence for this was readily available. In *Frontier* I attempted to provide an overview of the situation as I had come to see it:

> Frontier society bristled with guns. Men – and sometimes women as well – carried guns when out of doors and kept them loaded and close to hand at home. When anxiety intensified they were put under the pillow or beside the bed, were grasped in the night at the slightest unexplained sound and were picked up again when venturing out in the morning. In

some places this routine was followed for months, or even years on end.

This situation was true of the old pastoral districts which Ward saw as the forcing ground for the growth of distinctive national habits and sentiments. When the Leslie brothers pushed up onto the Darling Downs in 1840 the expedition took 'plenty of firearms for fear of the blacks'. Macmillan's party which travelled south into Gippsland at much the same time was heavily armed. Each member had two double-barrelled guns, a brace of pistols and sixty rounds of ammunition for each gun. They were instructed to have the guns beside them in camp covered with their blankets 'to be ready at a moment's warning'. On a frontier cattle station in Queensland visited by the explorer Leichhardt in 1840 one man kept watch continually, gun in hand, while there were nearly a dozen other guns in the corner of the hut ready for use. On the Ovens River in that same year, shepherds would not leave the head station without being provided with a shotgun and a brace of pistols. A pioneer of the Port Phillip frontier recalled in later years: 'the blacks being so tretchrous it took us to be washful to ourselves, for no one durst steer out without a loaded gun in his hand [*sic*]' .

This was true of every colony and almost all districts. If anything, pioneers in northern Australia in the late nineteenth century and early twentieth century were more heavily, and certainly more effectively, armed than their counterparts in the southern colonies in the early colonial period. How did a fine, creative historian like Russel Ward not see, not notice the pistols nonchalantly thrust through the belt of his noble frontiersman, the carbine slung across the shoulder, the abundant ammunition, the bloodstained hands? How did he miss something so obvious? How did Australia itself forget the truth about pioneering around the vast frontiers? One answer is that an unexpurgated account of settlement robs the bushman of his glamour. He becomes a far less attractive and decidedly more sinister figure once the Aborigines are brought back into the story. His nobility can only be sustained in their absence. His innocence can only be maintained for as long as the witnesses for the prosecution are kept out of court.

And what do we do with the still-common proposition that the frontier was the forcing ground of national values and characteristics, or the more generalised version of the same idea that the bush is the 'real Australia'? This view was developed at a time when the Aborigines were exiled from the story of the nation. With their return the situation changes. We immediately notice the dual role of the nomad tribe. They certainly were, as Ward and many others observed, members of an itinerant rural working class. But they were also part of a caste of racial overlords forcing submission from a recently conquered and dispossessed underclass. I'm not at all sure we can attribute the admired bush values of egalitarianism, mateship solidarity and anti-authoritarianism to the first role and deny any link at all with the second. The ubiquitous presence of the 'subject race' enhanced in a way not possible otherwise the equality of all whites, who were not black. The use and abuse of Aboriginal women added to the sense of mateship. Mates shared black women with their fellows – and were expected to do so in a way that would not have happened with white women, other than prostitutes. Shared sex without affection or responsibility strengthened male bonding. Complicity in atrocity, abuse and abduction added greatly to the sense of solidarity. When race was the issue all white men stuck together, boss and worker, bond and free, Protestant and Roman. Nothing more strengthened anti-authoritarianism than the profound division between the city and the bush over how the blacks should be treated. Nothing government did called forth more contempt and greater resistance than the endeavour to bring white men to justice for murdering blacks. And on no other issue was anti-authoritarianism so successful as with this one. It is not clear that it should be seen as something that as a nation we should celebrate.

Looking back now over twenty years I can see that I reacted in complex ways as I saw the new stories undermining the old. I felt that my generation of Australians should have been told the truth about the border wars; about the pioneers' complicity in murder, abduction and rape; about the fear and hatred; about the way Australia was acquired. I thought we should have been presented with a morally complex story, not one of facile triumphalism. It should have been tragic rather than vainglorious. I think we could have dealt with that and in the process found Australian history both more challenging and more engaging. I don't think we just wanted to be relaxed and comfortable about the past. We knew we were no longer British. We needed to know who we were and where we had come from.

X

*Confronting the Myth of
Peaceful Settlement*

My extensive research into frontier conflict led me on inevitably
into a series of confrontations with many deeply embedded, and
often dearly cherished, assumptions about the Aborigines, about
the settlers, about the process of colonisation, about Australian
history as a whole. They included the idea that the Aborigines
were a uniquely peaceful, unwarlike people who offered no resistance to European incursion; that the settlers were able to
occupy Australia without conflict; that ideas of warfare, conquest
and invasion were, therefore, inappropriate for local circumstances. These assumptions were difficult to grapple with
because they had been around for such a long time and were part
of the image which very many people had of Australia. They were
also appealing proposals which the community could not be
expected to relinquish without a struggle. My research into
earlier historical works indicated the strength and endurance of
many of these ideas. The more I read the more I realised that

I was in conflict with assumptions that I had grown up with. The most immediate and obvious point of contention was the question of peaceful settlement.

As I read my way through the work of earlier historians I realised that the idea that Australia had been uniquely free of conflict could be traced back to some of the earliest books written on the subject. A history of New South Wales published in 1816 claimed that the early settlers had not 'established themselves by the sword, nor willingly done injury to the naked miserable stragglers, who were found on these barren shores'. Sixty years later another history of the continent repeated the claim. Australia, the author declared, was not founded in bloodshed. Indeed the records showed that there had been nothing more than 'progressive sheep farming, never armed conflict with the inhabitants'. Australia presented a 'happy contrast' to colonisation of the Americas or of Africa. In fact 'no grander victory of Peace has this world ever witnessed than the acquisition of Australasia by the British nation'. Again in 1924 a general survey of Australian history made the same assessment: Australia was the 'only country' which had been acquired by 'peaceful occupation'; it had 'known no wars within its boundaries'.

There were of course many historians writing between 1816 and 1924 who did not make such claims to uniqueness. But few fully accounted for violence on the frontier. They distanced themselves from it by writing of it as something which belonged to the earliest days of settlement, to the era of absolute governors and convicts and redcoats. And this was the way I had thought of it and taught about it in my first year at the University College. As we have seen, the books which virtually wrote the Aborigines out of the story also wrote out the violence. They engaged in expurgation

136

by omission. Another common way of dealing with the question of frontier conflict was to relate peaceful settlement to mild and unwarlike Aborigines who either couldn't or wouldn't resist the incoming Europeans. This interpretation, I found from my reading, also had a long history.

In articles published in a Sydney newspaper in the early 1850s, and republished in book form in 1888, R.J. Flanagan argued that the Aborigines had made no impression on colonial society. He explained why:

> This, no doubt, is in great measure owing to that physical inferiority which this people certainly exhibit in as great a degree as any other race of men known. Their isolated and scattered position, their roving mode of life, their unwarlike character, their rude and all but harmless weapons, the utter absence of anything like concert in their habits and operations, have ever rendered them unimportant neighbours and feeble and insignificant enemies. Incapable of creating any considerable mischief, they have never, by war or by their opposition to the progress of the white man, forced themselves on the attention of either the government or philanthropists of Europe.

I found that many twentieth-century scholars took up the substance of Flanagan's assessment, that his ideas remained current for a long time. In his famous book *Australia*, published in 1930, W.K. Hancock argued that Aboriginal society had been 'pathetically helpless' when assailed by the colonists. Two years later the distinguished anthropologist Raymond Firth wrote that the Aborigine reacts in a simpler manner to invasion than do the

Maoris or Melanesians: 'he mutely dies'. It was a view that was still common in historical works in the 1960s, repeated in the comments of Russel Ward and J.M.H. Ward. The idea of a peaceful and passive people obviously appealed to many different people for a wide range of reasons. It could be linked to the idea of Aboriginal inferiority – they lacked the will, courage and/or intelligence to resist. It supported the view that Australia had a uniquely peaceful history; that as a people, we were remarkably slow to kill one another. But the same idea was taken up by those who wanted to condemn the Europeans for unpardonable and needless brutality towards an inoffensive people who in no way deserved their fate. Putative lack of aggression, while derided by some, was viewed by others as a sign of moral superiority or spiritual enlightenment.

A view still commonly expressed when I began writing about the frontier was that a major reason for the low status of Aborigines was that they hadn't earned the respect of white Australians by fighting for their land and their rights in the way that other indigenous people – the Maoris, Indians, Bantu – had done elsewhere in the world. They had, to some extent at least, brought ignominy on themselves. In 1972 the political scientist Colin Tatz compared race relations in Australia, New Zealand, Canada and South Africa and concluded that there was a direct correlation between the recognition of indigenous rights and the degree to which they fought against the colonists. He called this the 'respect factor' and implied that the Aborigines didn't measure up to the standards set by their counterparts in other countries. It was a view shared by the anthropologist K.R. McConochie. In the following year he suggested that settlers were likely to respect indigenous people 'if they put up a good fight'.

But did the Aborigines put up a good fight? Or were they pathetically helpless when reacting to the settlers?

My own research, and that of many other historians during the 1970s and 1980s, made certain things clear. Aboriginal society resisted the colonists in many different ways. Action was scattered and sporadic, and varied widely in intensity and effectiveness. A lot depended on the nature of the country in question, the number of encroaching settlers and the effectiveness of their weapons, which improved greatly during the course of the nineteenth century. Where the Europeans could use their horses unimpeded by terrain or vegetation, the Aborigines were at a grave disadvantage. It was difficult for them to coordinate resistance over large areas and the constant need to find food limited the capacity to bring large numbers together. In only a few places did Aboriginal attack hold settlement back or force the abandonment of districts already occupied. But despite the great disadvantages of their position the evidence from all over Australia establishes beyond doubt the considerable impact of resistance. This can be gauged from the reaction of Europeans, from the economic effects of Aboriginal action and by the deep fear which Aborigines evoked among frontier settlers.

My Tasmanian education taught me a little about the Black War and there seemed to be a general community recognition of the conflict which accompanied pioneer settlement. But because it was widely accepted that the Tasmanian Aborigines were extinct, past violence seemed to have little continuing relevance – like bushranging, it was one of the colourful aspects of 'the old days'. When I returned to Hobart to read the colonial newspapers and government records for the 1820s and 1830s, the great brutality of the Black War quickly became apparent. The conflict was carefully quantified by the distinguished Tasmanian scholar N.J.B. Plomley, who determined that between 1824 and 1831 there were 706 incidents in which the Aborigines attacked the colonists or their property. During those seven years 170 Europeans were killed, 200 were wounded and a further 225 were harassed or threatened in one way or another; 347 houses and huts were plundered or burnt. Equally detailed research has yet to be done in other parts of Australia and the information may not be so well recorded elsewhere. But the Tasmanian situation was by no means exceptional. In many frontier districts so many sheep and cattle were either killed or driven away that individuals were bankrupted and whole communities threatened with ruin. There were constant laments about the situation in colonial newspapers. In 1861 the Ipswich paper the *North Australian* declared:

> So injurious to the best interests of the colony do outrages by the blacks become, in deterring settlement and keeping out capital, that we look upon them as the worst evil of our position, and as the greatest barrier to the development of our resources. If there be in Queensland at the present moment one subject, which more than any other is of the highest importance . . . that subject is the better protection of frontier districts.

Twenty years later the same complaints were made about conditions in the north of the colony, the editor of the *Queenslander* observing:

> During the last four or five years the human life and property destroyed by the aboriginals in the North total up to a serious

amount . . . settlement on the land, and the development of
the mineral and other resources on the country, have been in
a great degree prohibited by the hostility of the blacks, which
still continues with undiminished spirit.

Similar sentiments were expressed all around the frontiers of
settlement – in Hobart, Launceston and Sydney in the 1820s, in
Darwin and the north of Western Australia in the 1910s and
1920s, and in many other places in between those dates.

Having been brought up on stories of heroic pioneers and
inoffensive or ineffectual Aborigines, I doubt if I ever gave any
thought to the great fear and gnawing anxiety of the many isolated parties of Europeans in danger of Aboriginal attack. Once
I began reading contemporary newspapers, letters and diaries I
found the evidence for them both abundant and ubiquitous. But
merely to state this fact did not seem to be enough to persuade
sceptical readers and listeners. What was required was evidence
from all parts of Australia and from many different people. A Tasmanian farmer observed in 1830 that the reaper in the field was
in constant dread, so much so that his work suffered because he
spent half his time 'looking about for fear of sudden attack'.
Island settlers who were compelled to travel away from their
properties on business 'left their families prey to inexpressible
anxiety' for fear that they would not return. On the Macintyre
River in northern New South Wales in 1840 the stockmen were
under siege, and for months on end 'not one of them could stir
from his hut unarmed; when one milked or went for a bucket of
water, another fully armed stood over him; the horses in the
paddocks were killed and the calves in the pen also close to the
huts where the men lived'. A central Queensland squatter told

a public meeting in Rockhampton in 1865 that he and his men had lived 'five years constantly in arms'. Selectors in North Queensland in the 1880s felt they were 'liable to be speared or tomahawked at any moment'. The miner working small isolated claims felt 'dogged and hemmed in on every side and his life menaced every time [he] set foot out of doors'.

There were no front lines in the 'border wars', no clear division of territory, no large and obvious bodies of combatants. The Aborigines knew the country and were able to move quickly and unpredictably, often at night. The settlers were never certain when they might appear. A Tasmanian frontiersman complained that Aboriginal movements were 'so uncertain and conducted with so much uncertainty and secrecy' that he seldom heard of them except when they suddenly appeared to commit 'acts of aggression and cruelty'. A fellow Tasmanian wrote anxiously: 'They are hovering close around us. I live in constant anxiety fearing some murder or dreadful accident'. A young Queensland squatter confided in his diary in 1863: 'As to the blacks one cannot tell how near they may be – an odd spear may at any unsuspecting moment be whizzed into one's "vitals".' In Western Australia in 1837 Bessie Bussell wrote that the word native was 'fraught with fatigue, fear and anxiety'. A pioneer venturing into new country in southern Queensland in the 1840s found that his men were 'frightened into convulsions', while in Brisbane Valley the squatters lived in 'perpetual suspense . . . ever on the tiptoe of expectation and indeed sometimes in a state of high mental tension'.

Having read so many accounts of anxiety and anguish, I came both to understand and sympathise with the plight of beleaguered pioneers, their own often violent response to the stress of the frontier notwithstanding. Fear rendered their violence much more explicable and their hatred more understandable. It made the pioneer far less heroic but much more human. In a sense, the image of the heroic frontiersman depended on the existence of inoffensive Aborigines. When reading the many accounts of settlers' fear – and especially their terror in the night – I was often reminded of the strange reaction of my neighbour who rang me in high anxiety about what he thought was a corroboree in the vacant block but then had to add that he wasn't frightened himself, only for the women and children. The reason for his reaction may have been the same one that has prevented Australian historians from dealing with white fear and anxiety. If you hold an adversary – or potential adversary – in very low regard then it becomes that much more difficult to admit to fear and anxiety or to allow such feelings in figures given heroic status in national mythology.

It was only slowly that I came to talk publicly about frontier conflict as being a kind of warfare. Bolder and more radical writers had done so before me. But the evidence I uncovered encouraged me to follow that example and to see the ways in which the Australian community had avoided taking this path. It was much more comforting to regard the Aborigines as criminals, and action against them as law enforcement. The approach of Paul Hasluck in his *Black Australians* is again instructive. He was aware that early governors made some references to fighting a war, but dismissed their comments as something of an aberration of early colonial society. 'This idea', he wrote:

> was one that belonged to the early phases of settlement when soldiers were charged with the protection of settlers and was incompatible with the police duty in later years. There was no idea of warfare in the northern settlements . . .

Police duty sounds so much more comforting than war. It also diminishes the significance and the political implications of Aboriginal resistance. Police action is all about maintaining order, not about conquest and expropriation.

However, those involved either directly or indirectly in frontier conflict constantly spoke and wrote of warfare. They did this in the early nineteenth century, as Hasluck observed, but they also did so in the middle and late nineteenth century and the early twentieth century. They talked of war on many occasions and in all parts of Australia in books and letters, speeches and sermons, public statements and private conversations. I carefully collected all this evidence on the assumption that it would eventually be needed to mount a challenge to such a powerful and appealing idea as peaceful colonisation. Within a few months of the arrival of the First Fleet, Governor Phillip and his officers were already talking about a 'state of petty warfare'. A few years later there were official references to 'open war' fought between the settlers and resident clans along the Hawkesbury. When conflict broke out in the Hunter Valley in 1826 a local missionary wrote back to his superiors in London to inform them that 'war has commenced and still continues against the Aborigines of this land'. A decade later, in northern New South Wales, the Europeans believed that the whole region was in 'a state of warfare' and that they were living in 'an enemy's country'.

Similar sentiments were expressed in Tasmania. The 'Black War' was the term used in the 1820s. Settlers writing to the government referred to 'a general and open warfare' in the interior, where Aboriginal action showed that they had determined on a 'declaration of war with the whites'. More significant was the response of the serving and retired soldiers in the Colony.

An ex-captain of the 64th Regiment believed the Big River tribe was 'at open war with the Colony'. The senior serving officer in the same district thought the conflict amounted to 'arduous warfare'. The Governor, Colonel George Arthur, referred to war many times in his official correspondence, variously writing of 'unpleasant warfare', 'a species of warfare of the most distressing kind', 'lawless warfare', 'lawless and cruel warfare', 'lamented and protracted warfare', 'warfare of the most dreadful description'.

There was much talk of warfare in the other colonies and later in the century. In Queensland in 1861 a member of Parliament declared that 'the people of this colony must be considered to be, as they always have been, at open war with the Aborigines'. The *Moreton Bay Courier* reported in 1852 that the Aborigines in the northern districts were 'in an actual state of warfare'. A correspondent writing to the same paper spoke of 'a secret war to the knife'. A prominent settler giving evidence to a Select Committee on the Native Police in 1861 referred to a 'kind of open war on the frontier'. In a letter to the *North Australian* in 1861 from the Peak Downs district, 'An Inhabitant of the Northern Districts' announced 'we are at war with the blacks'. In 1879 the editor of the *Queenslander* informed his readers 'we are today at open war with every tribe of wild blacks on the frontier'. A colleague writing for the *Queensland Figaro* referred to 'the constant border warfare on the verge line of settlement'.

Western Australia was no different. A naval officer visiting the Swan River in 1832 noted in his diary that the settlers were involved in 'a most awful warfare'. The military commandant of the colony at the time, F.C. Irwin, set out to bring an end to what he described as 'petty and harassing warfare'. His junior officer, Lieutenant Bunbury, thought he had been sent to the York district 'to make war upon the natives'. A settler concerned with the violence around the small settlement declared: 'We are at war with the original owners, we have never known them in any capacity but as enemies'. He continued:

> But if ye have taken their country from them, and they refuse to acknowledge your title to it, ye are at war with them; and, having never allowed your right to call them British subjects, they are justified by the usages of war in taking your property wherever they find it, and in killing you whenever they have an opportunity.

References to war were not, as Hasluck supposed, confined to the early period or to conflict in the south of Western Australia. In 1902 a member of Parliament told his colleagues that it was necessary to shoot the northern Aborigines for, after all, 'it was only a matter of warfare'. The state premier, the Hon. G. Leake, agreed, explaining to the parliament that when the Aborigines attacked the settlers and their property 'that is tantamount to a declaration of war'.

In my teaching I often referred to Aboriginal resistance as a form of guerrilla warfare. Some students were quite hostile to this idea. I was told on a number of occasions that my proposition must be wrong because Che Guevara and Mao Tse-tung had invented guerrilla war. More sophisticated critics took the view that to refer to Aboriginal resistance in that way was to impose contemporary views on the past. But the settlers realised that they were engaged in a specific type of war and wrote variously of 'a kind of war', 'a sort of warfare', 'a species of warfare'. They often referred to guerrilla warfare, a term which came out of the

Spanish campaign of the Napoleonic Wars, in which many early colonists had fought. A Western Australian settler referred in 1833 to the Aboriginal adoption of the 'guerilla mode of warfare'. A history of Tasmania written in 1835 referred to the difficulties of frontier settlers who were 'suffering from a guerilla war'. Governor Arthur clearly understood the problem of dealing with a fast-moving elusive enemy. 'They suddenly appear', he wrote, 'commit some act of outrage and then as suddenly vanish: if pursued it seems impossible to surround and capture them'. A writer in the *Hobart Town Courier* in 1830 understood that the Aborigines were employing the 'natural weapons' of their condition, 'the natural tactics of war with which providence has provided them'.

Some settlers advanced that argument even further. Having recognised that they were engaged in a form of warfare, they came to see the Aborigines as legitimate defenders of their homelands, as patriots and martyrs. A Tasmanian settler wrote to a local paper in 1828, observing that the Aborigines considered every injury they could inflict on the Europeans as 'an act of duty and patriotism'. It was 'absurd to see the blacks as "occasional rioters"', a colonist in New South Wales argued in 1839, because it was clear that they were 'enemies arrayed in arms and waging a war against Europeans as invaders'. The Government Resident in the Northern Territory observed in 1890 that reports from the outside country 'east and west' are that the blacks are 'beginning to understand the conditions under which the white man holds the country of which they consider they have been robbed'. After careful enquiry he was of the view that the Aborigines believed 'entrance into their country is an act of invasion. It is a declaration of war, and they will halt at no opportunity of attacking the white invader'.

The sophistication and cogency of assessments made long ago sometimes amazed me, as did their compelling contemporary relevance. Correspondents writing to the colonial newspapers as long ago as the 1820s presented arguments and insights which can still astound the modern reader. There was one letter which I have returned to and quoted from many times since I first found it in the poorly printed pages of the short-lived *Launceston Advertiser*. The anonymous correspondent asked, in 1831:

> Are these unhappy people, the subjects of our king, in a state of rebellion or are they an injured people, whom we have invaded and with whom we are at war?
>
> Are they within the reach of our laws; or are they to be judged by the law of nations?
>
> Are they to be viewed in the light of murderers, or as prisoners of war?
>
> Have they been guilty of any crime under the laws of nations which is punishable by death, or have they only been carrying on a war *in their own way*?
>
> Are they British subjects at all, or a foreign enemy who has never yet been subdued and which resists our usurped authority and domination?
>
> We are at war with them: they look upon us as enemies — as invaders — as oppressors and persecutors — they resist our invasion. They have never been subdued, therefore they are not rebellious subjects, but an injured nation, defending in their own way, their rightful possessions which have been torn from them by force.

Although written over 160 years ago, this letter is still challenging and disturbing, raising issues which even now have not been satisfactorily dealt with.

Such letters alerted me to other writers in other towns and in different times, who compared their own situation to colonists in other parts of the world who were involved in warfare. In Tasmania, as we have seen, the military officers compared the tactics of the Aborigines with the guerrillas they had observed in Spain during the Napoleonic Wars. In the late 1850s Queenslanders drew parallels with the Indian Mutiny, local papers observing that conflict in central Queensland had cost 'more white victims than the massacre at Cawnpore'. The Dawson River clans had committed atrocities 'only equalled by the Sepoys of India'. In 1861 a member of the Queensland House of Assembly told his colleagues that they must treat the Aborigines 'as a hostile tribe, as they did the New Zealanders'. In 1885 a North Queensland settler argued that local blacks were just as difficult to deal with 'as the savage hordes in Sudan'. A prominent settler in the Northern Territory argued before a select committee of the South Australian parliament in 1899 that conflict in Australia should be seen in a wider perspective because in other parts of the world it was 'looked upon as heroism . . . for a white man to conquer natives'. At much the same time a Western Australian settler excused punitive expeditions because participants were as justified as were British soldiers who 'shot at either Kaffirs, Zulus, Abyssinians or any other inferior race'. When the correspondent to the *Townsville Herald* with the nom de plume 'H7H' hit back at critics in a subsequent letter, he related his account of atrocity to the expansion of Empire. His story of violence and murder was:

> no more blood curdling than many accounts of battles fought
> by the Empire's forces in the Soudan and in Zululand, when

the British government was doing just what the squatter was doing in any case – simply acquiring property, or to put it another way, extending the Empire.

The view that the Aborigines were internal enemies with whom the settlers were at war carried over into discussions about colonial expenditure on external defence. 'We have not grudged a large outlay on national defence', the editor of the *Queenslander* observed in 1879, 'with but a very doubtful prospect of foreign attack'. Then why, he asked, does the government 'stint the funds necessary for the repression of the enemy within our gates'? It was a viewpoint popular out on the sprawling frontier. Writing in the same paper some years later, an embattled selector from a small farm on the Atherton Tableland argued that:

> there are thousands, that can be spent on Defence Forces, to protect the inhabitants of this country from the invisible, perhaps imaginary, but for certain distant enemies; but we cannot afford to keep an efficient body of police to keep in check the enemy we have at our door, the enemy of every day, the one that slowly but surely robs and impoverishes us.

After more than a decade of research and after reading the work of other historians, the story of settlement appeared to be dramatically different from the one that I grew up with and had seen confirmed in the books that I first used in my teaching – Scott's *Short History of Australia* and Greenwood's *Australia: A Social and Political History*. The Aborigines were far more important in the scheme of things than either book suggested. Colonists in the nineteenth century were fully aware of this and wrote and spoke endlessly about the 'aboriginal question'. Aboriginal resistance was much more challenging, prolonged and various than subsequent accounts allowed. It was crushed everywhere sooner or later, but it was spirited and determined and exacted a considerable cost in European lives and property and peace of mind. Violence was ever present along the ragged line of early interaction. At least 2000 Europeans and 20 000 Aborigines died violently and many more were wounded. Many Europeans came to the view that they were involved in a distinctive form of warfare and that the Aborigines were engaged in a perfectly understandable and totally legitimate defence of their territory against an invader. This view of the colonising venture can be found in the earliest debates on the matter in the 1820s. In one of the first letters on the subject in the Australian press, a correspondent using the nom de plume 'Zeno' wrote to the *Hobart Town Gazette* in July 1824:

> We ought to feel that we have invaded a domain from which our invasion has expelled those who were born, bred, and providentially supplied in it; that we have driven by our usurpation, families from their birth-place, and then completed our cruelty by destroying in sport, and consuming for profit, the principal means of their subsistence.

XI

Arguing about Invasion

'We ought to feel we have invaded a domain . . .'

It is an exhortation which many Australians refuse to heed.
Indeed, the concept of invasion has been strenuously resisted in
recent years as an unacceptable alternative to the traditional idea
of peaceful settlement. Powerful passions have been aroused by
the controversy; political leaders, media personalities and
prominent commentators have all had their say. The use of the
term invasion is seen by conservative intellectuals and politicians
as part of a much wider agenda often summarised as the 'black-
armband' version of history, the promotion of which the Prime
Minister, John Howard, called 'one of the more insidious developments in Australian political life over the past decade'. Geoffrey Blainey, who first coined the phrase 'black-armband
history', believes the effect of such historical revision would be
to divide the nation forever. Retired bureaucrat and senator John
Stone went even further, referring to 'evil forces' which were
working 'to falsify our history'. The suggestion is that to tamper

with history is to subvert the nation. Conservative commentator Ken Baker argued that to rewrite Australia's past 'as a story of destruction and persecution' would 'ultimately work to undermine the legitimacy of existing institutions inherited from the past'. Federal Opposition Leader John Hewson launched a fierce attack on the new history in December 1993, declaring that over recent years 'one particular version' of Australian history had gained ground and undue influence. It was, he believed, a dangerously distorted view of Australian history which was designed to divide the community. To those who held this view, the arrival of the British at Botany Bay was the beginning of the 'so-called "European occupation" of Australia and the start of a history in which there is more cause for guilt than pride'. Hewson urged his readers to fight back against a view of Australian history that judged the deeds of past generations 'on the basis of values and priorities held by some Australians today'.

Debate about the invasion arose during the Bicentennial year of 1988 in numerous locations, assuming various forms. Early in the year John Dawkins, the Federal Minister for Education, addressed the annual conference of the Australian Teachers Federation, telling them:

> It seems to me that we in Australia have a lot to be ashamed about in terms of our history and until we face up to the shame we cannot satisfactorily celebrate the past 200 years.

He said that it was necessary to recall that, in the past, history had been distorted and that it was the responsibility of the teaching profession to ensure that 'our black history was presented in a more accurate and positive way'.

Dawkins was quickly attacked. Shadow Education Minister Jim Carlton said that the suggestion that history had been distorted was deeply offensive:

> According to Mr Dawkins, Australian children should read history books that reflect a deep sense of shame on the part of all Australians over the treatment of Aborigines by their forebears.

Academics pounced on the Minister, accusing him of trying to force teachers to promote government propaganda. Particularly strident was the criticism from Professor Les Marchant, Head of the Centre for East Asian Studies at the University of Western Australia, who described the Dawkins speech as 'a fascist act of intellectual terrorism'.

But the teachers scarcely needed the advice of the Minister. The conference decided unanimously to urge members to boycott all Bicentenary functions and activities which did not address 'the Aboriginal perspective'. The Federation's Aboriginal Coordinator, Pat Fowell, declared: 'We are not talking about an embellishment or exaggeration of history, just the truth, as bloody and horrific as it is'.

The matter of invasion created problems in June 1988 for Sydney's Powerhouse Museum, which used the controversial word in several displays. In providing captions to go with Aboriginal artefacts the curators observed that only a few specimens had survived 'from before the European invasion' and that men and women had used different methods of fishing 'before the Europeans invaded'. A member of the public objected and wrote to the relevant minister in the state government, Peter Collins, who sent the letter on to the Museum where it was considered by the Board of Trustees. They decided that all reference to 'invade' and 'invasion' should be deleted. But the Board was clearly divided on the question. One member observed that invasion was an emotive word and was 'contrary to the community views', while another remarked that 'If it was white people whose society was overturned we would have called it an invasion'. The Museum's Acting Director defended the decision, explaining that removing the offending words was in the interests of 95 per cent of the public and that 'a lot of elderly visitors find it hard to understand that there might have been a change of attitude to white settlement in Australia'. But the ban did not last twenty-four hours. Next day the Acting Director was reported as saying that the controversial labels would remain, 'in the interests of public debate'.

But resistance to the use of 'invasion' was much more effective in Queensland in February 1994, when controversy broke out over a new social studies curriculum guide prepared for teachers in state primary schools. It was a controversy in which I became directly involved.

In 1991 the curriculum branch of the Education Department decided to review social studies teaching material and bring it into line with departmental policies on social justice and equity. After extensive consultations new sourcebooks were produced which provided a much more 'accurate portrayal of the cultures and history of Aboriginal and Torres Strait Islander peoples'. A number of key generalisations informed the new material. Among them were that Australia had been invaded and that the effects had been 'devastating to the population of Aboriginal people and Torres Strait Islander people'.

The document also included a Teacher Information Sheet concerning appropriate terminology, setting out preferred and unsuitable words. 'Non-indigenous exploration and occupation' was recommended to replace such terms as 'discover', 'pioneers', 'explorers'. The preferred terms recognised that Australia was already explored and known to Aboriginal and Torres Strait Islander people. 'Discover', 'pioneers' and 'explorers' were words which implied the non-existence of indigenous people. 'Invasion' was favoured because 'settlement' suggested that no-one was living in the country before the coming of the Europeans. In a separate section on invasion teachers were urged to point out to students that the imperial government did not ask permission from the indigenous people to take over their land, did not negotiate a treaty with or pay any compensation to any of the original occupants of Australia, and engaged in various forms of violence to establish colonies in different parts of Australia. At the end of the section teachers were encouraged to refer students to the dictionary definition of invasion and then to:

> Ask them to consider whether, given the information they now have, Aboriginal people and Torres Strait Islander people were invaded. Students could engage in a formal debate on this question.

Long before any debate could take place in the classrooms of Queensland, the curriculum material became the focal point for controversy which drew in politicians, media personalities and ordinary citizens throughout Queensland and then in the rest of Australia as well.

The Shadow Minister for Education declared bluntly:

'White people came out here and settled and that is it'. Opposition Leader Rob Borbidge said it was a disgrace to the explorers, pioneers and settlers to have their efforts dismissed simply to conform with the Labor government's 'politically correct rewrite' of history. The *Courier-Mail* ran stories with headlines like:

Explorers Axed in 'Correct' Syllabus
Furore Over Invasion

The Education Minister, Pat Comben, ruled out any political directive to change the material but a day later was overruled by Premier Goss, the *Courier-Mail* headlines declaring:

Goss Cans Invasion Textbook

The Premier ordered that the handbook be rewritten, declaring that terms like invasion went too far. There was, he remarked:

a world of difference between the arrival of the First Fleet and what most people understand as an invasion. I think that just about all Australians would not regard what happened in 1788 as an invasion.

Goss killed the offending book but in doing so enlivened the debate. Aboriginal organisations in Queensland expressed outrage. A group of academics from the University of Queensland wrote an open letter to the Premier insisting that the term invasion was 'entirely accurate and appropriate'. Radio personality John Laws ridiculed the curriculum planners and praised 'Goss the boss'. On his program on 9 February he declared:

> But the word invasion is inaccurate when we're referring to landing of British people here in Australia . . . I mean it's divisive, it's setting the Aboriginal and white people against each other. Did we enter as an enemy? We came as friends . . . Why are we talking about invasion, resistance, dispossession and genocide?

The editor of the *Australian* observed in similar vein:

> Nobody doubts that killings and violence occurred as a result of the interaction between the Europeans and Aborigines in Australia. Nobody doubts that the full extent of the injustice done to the Aboriginal people must be recognised.

But to teach schoolchildren that Australia began with an invasion, 'pure and simple', would only 'compound our difficulties'. Most Australians, he argued, would never accept 'the denial of the legitimacy of their civilisation which the term invasion implies'.

The debate about invasion flared again in New South Wales later in June 1994. The Minister for Education, Virginia Chadwick, had come out in favour of using terms like invasion during the Queensland debate. She was sharply criticised by the state National Party conference in May for facilitating a process that was 'changing the written history of Australia'. The local branch of the Teachers Federation reacted strongly, urging members to ban the teaching of any Australian history or social science subject which failed to acknowledge that Australia was invaded in 1788.

The Senior Vice-President of the Federation, Denis Fitzgerald, declared:

> We regard this in the same way as we regard Creationism. We do not want to teach a sanitised view of Australian history. We believe we have a professional responsibility not to teach something that is distorted or untruthful.

This was too much for John Howard. In an article in the *Sunday Telegraph* with the headline 'Teacher "Thuggery" Distorts History', he accused the Federation of attempting to distort history to make a 'contemporary political point'. Members of the Federation were guilty of 'ideologically driven intellectual thuggery'.

When becoming involved in the debate myself, it seemed that the greatest fault with the argument of John Howard and many other conservative commentators was their assumption that any idea of invasion was a recent imposition on the facts of history, a fashionable ruse adopted by malcontents for blatantly political ends. In fact the story was quite different. There were observers in Britain who talked about invasion before the First Fleet sailed for Australia. Invasion was a word commonly used by colonists to understand and describe what they saw going on around them. This was true of New South Wales and Tasmania in the 1820s and 1830s and of Queensland and the Northern Territory fifty or sixty years later.

Soon after the announcement of the impending expedition to Australia, a correspondent writing to the London *Morning Herald* made the obvious point that the history of European colonisation gave little confidence in the outcome at the antipodes; it showed how 'improbable it is that any plantation can be made . . . without a cruel disregard for the lives of the natives'. Because they would be 'justly and naturally jealous of such invasion' they would ultimately be destroyed by the 'armed force which is sent out with the convicts, to support the occupancy of land not their own'. The perception of an invasion remained alive in Britain and was expressed by people who might be thought unlikely to hold such views. The highly respectable governors of the Van Diemen's Land Company wrote to their Tasmanian manager in 1830 reminding him that company employees 'ought to feel that we have invaded a domain from which our invasion has expelled those who were born, bred, and providentially supplied in it'. Writing at much the same time, Colonel C. J. Napier, one of Britain's most famous and celebrated soldiers, observed that the Tasmanians made a most courageous resistance to the invasion of the English.

Up until the 1830s British officials in both England and the colonies wrote as though Aborigines were a foreign enemy. Lord Bathurst, Secretary of State for the Colonies, instructed the governors of both New South Wales and Van Diemen's Land in 1825 that, when the Aborigines attacked the settlers, they should 'oppose force by force, and to repel such Aggressions in the same manner as if they proceeded from subjects of an accredited State'. When martial law was declared in Tasmania in 1830 the Solicitor General explained that it placed the Aborigines 'on the footing of open enemies to the King, in a state of actual warfare against him'.

The colonists themselves often spoke and wrote of conquest and invasion although there were, no doubt, many who disapproved of such terms. A correspondent wrote to the *Sydney Gazette* in August 1824 admonishing those who complained about Aboriginal attacks and arguing:

If we do not approve of their conduct in molesting our people or property, how can we approve of our conduct, in having first invaded their land, and, in great measure, deprived them of their pleasure and subsistence.

A few years later a Tasmanian settler raised the same questions about conquest, resistance and war. The Aborigines, he argued:

were originally the rightful owners and possessors of the island . . . The British Colonists have taken their country from them by force, they have persecuted them, wantonly sacrificed them . . . We are at war with them: they look upon us as enemies – as invaders – as their oppressors and persecutors – they resist our invasion.

Such sentiments were not confined to Tasmania, where there was a strong perception that a war had been fought. In Queensland the colonists frequently justified their actions with appeals to the cruel necessity of conquest, a correspondent in the *Moreton Bay Courier* asserting that 'if we hold this country by the right of conquest' and if that right gives us a just claim to its continual possession, then 'we must be empowered to enforce our claim by the strong arm whenever necessary . . .' 'It must be constantly borne in mind', the editor of the *Queensland Guardian* wrote in 1861, that with the white man 'it is a question of forced occupation or none at all'. His colleague on the *Port Denison Times* explained that the settlers 'as invaders' had to impose their laws upon the conquered. The Western Australian barrister E.W. Landor spoke out forcefully against what he called the 'amiable sophistry' that the British claim to Australia

was based on a right of occupancy. Why not, he thundered
in 1847:

> say boldly at once, a right of power? We have seized upon the
> country, and shot down the inhabitants, until the survivors
> have found it expedient to submit to our rule. We have acted
> as Julius Caesar did when he took possession of Britain. But
> Caesar was not so hypocritical as to pretend any moral *right*
> to possession . . . We have right to our Australian posses-
> sions; but it is the right of Conquest, and we hold them with
> the grasp of Power. Unless we proceed on this foundation,
> our conduct towards the native population can be considered
> only as a monstrous absurdity.

Many of the Europeans who had close contact with the
Aborigines, or who knew of the conditions on the frontier,
were convinced that it was a general view among the clans that
they were facing an invasion. After many months of contact
with the Tasmanian tribes George Augustus Robinson concluded that they had a 'tradition amongst them that the white
men have usurped their territory, have driven then into the
forest, have killed their game . . .' The young military officer
Lieutenant William Darling, who spent many months on the
Bass Strait Islands with the exiled Tasmanians, concluded that
they considered they had been 'engaged in a justifiable war
against the Invaders of their Country'. Sixty years later and at
the other end of the continent the Government Resident for the
Northern Territory expressed similar views. After careful
enquiry he was of the view that the Aborigines thought entrance
into their country 'an act of invasion'. It was a 'declaration of

war' and they would stop at no opportunity 'of attacking the white invaders'.

It would be possible to come up with many more examples of what Australian colonists had to say about the vexed questions of war, invasion and conquest. But it is clear that far from being a contemporary imposition on the past, the reverse is true. What we are seeing is merely the most recent upsurge of a debate that has been going on since the departure of the First Fleet. If political correctness was involved in the matter at all it was in the suppression of these questions by nationalist historians writing between 1900 and 1960, who were more interested in telling heroic tales than in confronting the legal and ethical problems underlying the process of colonisation. Many contemporary Australians still prefer the 'amiable sophistry' of peaceful settlement.

Commentators and politicians who object to the term invasion refer to particular aspects of the first settlement of 1788 to clinch their argument. They point to the fact that Governor Phillip was instructed to treat the Aborigines with 'amity and kindness'. While that is true it is scarcely persuasive. Such phrases were commonplace in instructions given to British explorers and to those of other European empires. Two hundred years earlier Philip II of Spain informed expeditions sailing for the Americas that he did not 'wish to give occasion or pretext for force or injury to the Natives'. But such benign intentions could only survive if the society being invaded acquiesced in its own conquest. Resistance to the European would lead irresistibly to violent repression. Governor Phillip's decision in December 1790 to send out fifty troops to strike universal terror into the Aboriginal clans – both those who were to suffer and those who would witness the punishment – was an inevitable consequence of settlement itself. The pleas of innocence on behalf of the officers of the First Fleet scarcely do them justice. They realised the nature of the enterprise and that the Aborigines were bound to resist encroachments on their land. David Collins, Phillip's secretary and senior legal officer in the colony, observed:

> While they entertain the idea of our having dispossessed them of their residences, they must always consider us as enemies; and upon this principle they made a point of attacking the white people whenever opportunity and safety concurred.

Other common arguments are no more persuasive – that the Aborigines did not resist the first landing or that the arrival of the First Fleet was nothing like such well-known invasions as the Normans in Britain in 1066 and the Germans in Russia in 1941. But there must be as many types of invasion as there are kinds of war. The fact is that the British arrived unannounced and uninvited with what was, in the circumstances, irresistible force, and consciously and officially claimed sovereignty over half the continent. They did not have a large army, but they calculated correctly they didn't need one. They had as much military power as was required for the job; cost-conscious administrators were scarcely likely to provide more. But the calculation about how many troops were required to meet any challenge from the Aborigines was openly discussed. In 1789 Governor Phillip wrote to his superiors in London informing them that 500 troops would be sufficient for the task. 'It will appear to your Lordship', he wrote:

after what has been said of the natives, that a less force will be wanted for the security of the settlement than what I considered as necessary soon after my arrival in this country, although that was not considerable . . . I presume that a battalion of 500 men will be sufficient, which will admit of one hundred being detached for the security of Norfolk Island.

When I became involved in the debate about the Queensland social studies curriculum I argued that if you arrive without being invited in another country and you bring military force with you with the intention of using that force to impose your will, then 'it has to be interpreted by any measure as an invasion'. I think terms like invasion and conquest are appropriate for what happened in Australia. That was what many colonists thought in the past and the evidence does seem to confirm the case. But I don't think the words 'settle' or 'settlement' or 'settlers' should be abandoned. The British arrived not with the idea of simply ruling over a subject race but of farming land, building houses and planning towns. Invasion and conquest prepared the way for settlement. Many pioneers who took up land played no direct part in the conquest and those who came into the colonies after the 'killing times' benefited from what had gone on before, but might not even have known much about it.

A more intriguing question is why so many Australians are defensive about the past, so sensitive to matters which were debated openly and robustly in the nineteenth century by people who were actually involved in the process of dispossession. It seems that many Australians want to enjoy both all the benefits brought by conquest and the untroubled conscience that would spring from a peaceful settlement. They have difficulty with the gritty and tough-minded realism of the pioneer settlers, men like Alexander Harris, who observed in 1847 that it was:

> a simple question of *intimidation* (nothing more) between the musket and the spear. And every black's commonsense solves this question so readily and correctly and uniformly, that the simple consciousness of its being the true and only question is sufficient at any time to bring them into a state of submission. And if we want more than that; if we want a league of peace on equal grounds, really there is no road to it but that we give up their land and forsake the country; for this and this only is the true source of aggravation . . . The blacks cannot be conciliated unless by giving up their country.

XII

Lest We Forget

A few years ago I was approached by members of a German television crew who were making a documentary in Tasmania. They
wanted to interview me about something they found very hard to
understand. They explained that they had been filming in the far
north-west corner of the island and had been told by numerous
people about a massacre of Aborigines at Cape Grim in the early
1830s. All the locals seemed to know the story. But the
German producer could not persuade any of them to talk about
it on camera. So they sought me out to explain why it was that
Australians still had such difficulty in coming to terms with
events that had occurred so long ago. After all, they said, we
Germans have had to reconcile ourselves with many far worse
things that are still within living memory. Why is it that you are
so sensitive about the past?

It seemed to me to be a very pertinent question, although I
don't think I made a very good job of answering it. Even when
Australians are willing to concede that Aborigines were badly

treated in the past they are uneasy about the detail, about looking too closely at things and pinning actual events down in time and place. Attempts to locate and mark sites of massacre have frequently been strenuously resisted in the communities in question. The same uneasiness is apparent when it is suggested that settlers and Aborigines were engaged in a form of warfare. The new Minister with responsibility for reconciliation, Philip Ruddock, told an ABC radio audience, in one of his first public appearances in his new role in October 1998, that there could not be a treaty between settler Australia and indigenous Australia because there had never been a war in this country. No doubt many people shared the Minister's view. But that should not encourage us to avoid a rigorous examination of where that proposition leads us.

If, as Minister Ruddock argued, there was no war, how can we explain the bloodshed, how can we account for the bodies? If Aborigines did not die in long-drawn-out, low-level, sporadic warfare then they must have been murdered. There doesn't seem to be any other explanation. They were not executed by the state as a result of the operation of the law except in those few situations where martial law was declared. They were killed singly or in groups in every part of the country. Their killers were soldiers, police troopers, both black and white, and private settlers. If there was no war then thousands of colonists were murderers and thousands more were accessories to murder. The whole of colonial society was complicit in the killing, governments and the courts failing on a massive scale to enforce the law and bring the murderers to justice.

Why should we consider this a more attractive way of seeing frontier conflict than viewing it as a kind of war? The proposition also runs headlong into the widespread indigenous view of the matter. Aborigines are certain they were engaged in warfare and lost their land as a consequence of defeat in war. That should occasion no surprise. What other possible ways of seeing the situation exist? Should they accept the views of the ex-Premier of Queensland, Joh Bjelke-Petersen, as expressed in 1998 to an English newspaper, that the Aborigines were the 'most lucky lucky people in the world' because 'we fought and died for this country, not them'? Should they agree with the assertion of the distinguished historian W.K. Hancock, who said in 1930 that Aborigines were 'pathetically helpless' when confronted by Europeans? Are Aborigines likely to look with favour on the common view that they were unable or unwilling to do anything to defend their land and way of life; that they were criminals or savages under the sway of primitive emotions? It is not surprising that Aborigines refuse to accept any of these interpretations of their behaviour crafted by Europeans over the years. And that makes the position taken by Minister Ruddock particularly problematic. Without some reconciliation of stories, some convergence of histories, it is hard to see how the broader agenda of reconciliation can be advanced. Is reconciliation possible between two peoples who fundamentally disagree about their shared past, who differ widely in their explanation of the reason why things are as they now are?

During my years of research into frontier conflict I was frequently forced to think about the nature of warfare. I lived in a garrison town. The military was ever present. The Lavarack Army Base was adjacent to the university. Platoons in full battle gear marched back and forth along the road to the university. Armed personnel carriers thundered through the streets; military helicopters whirred overhead. We took our young children to marches, to open days at the barracks, to more Anzac Day celebrations than I had ever been to in my life, where I was often deeply moved despite myself. Much was being written at the time about colonial resistance to imperial powers and about guerrilla warfare. But beyond all of these things there was the ever-growing weight of evidence about the extent, duration and ubiquity of frontier conflict and the often-expressed conviction of many colonists that they were engaged in warfare with the Aborigines.

I tried to deal with the implications of seeing frontier conflict as warfare in 1981, in the conclusion of *The Other Side of the Frontier*. I was particularly struck by the problem of how Australia should deal with those who had died in our own internal conflict given that the fallen warrior loomed so large in national rhetoric and iconography. I began with a simple question:

> How, then, do we deal with the Aboriginal dead? White Australians frequently say 'all that' should be forgotten. But it will not be. It cannot be. Black memories are too deeply, too recently scarred. And forgetfulness is a strange prescription coming from a community which has revered the fallen warrior and emblazoned the phrase 'Lest We Forget' on monuments throughout the land. If the Aborigines are to enter our history 'on terms of most perfect equality', as Thomas Mitchell termed it, they will bring their dead with them and expect an honoured burial. So our embarrassment is compounded. Do we give up our cherished ceremonies or do we make room for the Aboriginal dead on our memorials, cenotaphs, boards of honour and even in the pantheon of national heroes? If we are to continue to celebrate the

sacrifice of men and women who died for their country can
we deny admission to fallen tribesmen?

I realised from people's reactions to the book that for some
this was a deeply disturbing issue. They often singled this para-
graph out when discussing the book with me. I remember one
such reader particularly vividly. I met him at a reception at the
Institute for Commonwealth Studies in London. I had just delivered a lecture for the Menzies Centre for Australian Studies. The
gathering was highly respectable, well heeled, well connected. I
was approached by a man who introduced himself as the grandson
of one of the most significant of North Queensland's pioneers.
His was a name to be conjured with. I assumed he would have
taken a dim view of my lecture, which was about Aborigines in
Australian historical literature. He said he had read *The Other Side
of the Frontier*. I cringed, thinking he would strongly disapprove of
my views and dress me down for them. But he surprised me and
said, 'Reynolds, I have read your book and do you know, there is
something you said that I can't get out of my mind. It's on page
201. It's where you ask what are we going to do with the Aboriginal dead. That is the question, isn't it?'

I have returned to that question myself when speaking to
audiences in many parts of Australia recently on the question of
reconciliation and history. It is obvious that people are both
intensely interested in and deeply troubled by it. I talked about
the war dead in a lecture in Hobart in September 1998 and
returned to Hobart about six weeks later. On that second visit a
woman approached me and explained that she had been at my
earlier lecture and that she had not been able to put the question
out of her head. She said that she had asked all her friends and

acquaintances what they thought should happen about the legacy of the 'border wars' but that none of them had been able to come up with an answer. She said the question so disturbed her that she felt sick in the stomach whenever she thought about it.

Soon after that discussion the whole issue was resurrected by the Governor-General, Sir William Deane, when launching the book *Sacred Places: War Memorials in the Australian Landscape* by historian Professor Ken Inglis. Sir William observed that there were no memorials, 'at least of an official kind, to the Aborigines who were slaughtered in the black wars' of the colonial era. In his book Ken Inglis observed that 'monuments missing in a landscape can be as significant as those erected'. Australia in 1900 was almost bare of testimony to the 'most persistent of war-like encounters in the continent, contests for territory between old and new inhabitants'. At the launch Inglis argued that the Australian War Memorial must recognise these warlike encounters between black and white. It would present the Memorial board with the challenge and the opportunity to make a distinctive contribution to the task of reconciliation.

Controversy followed, with participants lining up both for and against the proposition. The Australian National University's Professor Ann Curthoys argued that it was essential for frontier conflict to be commemorated at the Memorial. 'White Australians', she noted, 'like to remember their own suffering in war but not that of indigenous Australians'. Similar sentiments were expressed by contributors who wrote to the newspapers. One correspondent to the *Australian* thought the conflict should be seen as war, both to establish that the continent was taken by force 'but also to get away from the emphasis on Aboriginal people as the helpless victims of massacre'. It was high time, he believed, that this aspect of our past became 'more fully accepted and appropriately commemorated and widely understood by young Australians', who could 'try to make amends for the past by fostering reconciliation between Aboriginal Australians and themselves'.

Another correspondent commented that every Anzac Day she felt the same thing: 'Where can I go to honour my fellow Australians who died resisting the European invasion?' In a long article in the *Australian*, Nicholas Rothwell canvassed various views on the question and concluded that a war memorial did much more than recognise that something very like a war took place in Australia during the settlement era. It pointed the way towards 'a salutary new public conception of the Aboriginal people. You fight wars against enemies. You defeat them, rather than writing their struggles out of your history.'

Spokesmen for the Returned Services League were predictably hostile to the proposition. The same line was taken by editorial writers in the major newspapers. The *Courier-Mail* argued that, while it was important to recognise the extent of frontier conflict, the War Memorial was not an appropriate place to commemorate it because it served a 'different purpose, commemorating the unity and sacrifice of the nation as a whole' in international wars. The editorial writer in the *Australian* thought that non-Aboriginal Australians were 'a long way from accepting the revisionist view of colonial conflicts' and any attempt to force the issue would sidetrack the progress towards reconciliation. The Queensland academic Glen St John Barclay took a similar position, arguing that the fragile plant of reconciliation would be damaged by the outrage which would be evoked by 'diverting the Australian War Memorial from its original purpose by making a memorial to shame, as well as to honour'. The Prime Minister joined the fray, arguing that because Australia was settled rather than conquered a state of war never existed and so there was no reason for any commemoration.

The controversy aroused by the question of the Aboriginal war dead should not come as a surprise. War is central to the experience of nationhood. Death in war is seen as the ultimate sacrifice for the nation. The fallen are revered as martyrs who gave up their lives for the benefit of the community. But the situation becomes complicated when white Australia seeks to incorporate indigenous Australia within the nation, when national leaders proclaim we are all members of one nation. If that is so then the logic is inescapable – we must treat the Aboriginal dead with as much respect and as much honour as we treat our own. Nothing less will do.

Clearly this has never been done, perhaps never even contemplated. It is therefore instructive to consider what would have happened if more than 20 000 colonists had died in Australia defending the nation against an invader. The deaths clearly would not have been forgotten or written out of history books. Battle sites would be known, remembered and commemorated. Monuments would grace many of them. A national day would, in all likelihood, have been declared to mark the sacrifice. Children would be told the old stories of loss, suffering and heroism, and encouraged to keep the memories of the martyrs alive.

It is not clear how indigenous communities would like us to remember the killing times. There would no doubt be differing views. Many people would probably think that it is a matter for the whitefellas to deal with. But some things are certain. They don't think we should pretend the killing times never occurred. They expect us to tell the truth and think we should be able to come to terms with it. They would also expect us to treat the war with the seriousness it warrants. To accept that it was conflict which determined the whole course of the history of the continent and was a precondition for the success of the colonising venture – a series of events as important as anything else that has occurred since the first European beachhead was established at Sydney in 1788.

Can settler Australia accommodate the indigenous interpretation of the past? Do white Australians want to do so? The project is central to the reconciliation process. The stated objective of the Reconciliation Council is to give to all Australians a 'shared ownership of their history'. But is this a realistic objective? The controversy about the War Memorial suggests that it may not be. Australians are also uneasy and ambivalent about the 'scars in the landscape', those known sites of multiple deaths where significant numbers of Aborigines were killed by the settlers. Aboriginal communities usually know the location of such haunted places. The map of the country is sprinkled with European names carrying a sinister message – Murdering Plains, Skull Creek, Murderer's Creek, Blood-Hole, Fighting Hills, Fighting Waterholes, Slaughterhouse Creek, Murdering Island.

A few monuments marking such spots have had a troubled history. A brass plate on a jarrah tree on the site of the 1834 Battle of Pinjarra, south of Perth, was stolen one night and the tree set on fire. A monument to the Kalkadoon people of north-west Queensland was unveiled in 1984, the centenary of conflict with the Native Police at Battle Mountain. The plaque referred to the event, 'one of Australia's historical battles of resistance against a paramilitary force of European settlers and the Queensland Native Mounted Police'. Since 1984 the monument has been frequently shot at and was eventually blown up. In 1991 the Yugambeh people of the Gold Coast – Beaudesert district in southern Queensland built a monument of their own at the Jebbribillum bora ring at Burleigh Heads. It commemorated the tribal members who had died defending their country either against the settlers in the colonial period or as members of Australia's armed forces in overseas wars.

One of the most interesting recent developments in relation to commemoration was the amendment of the monument set up on the Fremantle Esplanade in 1913 to mark the death of three pioneers fifty years before. In 1864 Frederick Panter, James Harding and William Goldmeyer were killed by Aborigines at Lagrange Bay in the north of the colony. A punitive expedition led by Maitland Brown retrieved the bodies and killed an unknown number of Aborigines in revenge. The monument paid tribute to the three dead explorers:

> Earliest explorers after Grey and Gregory of this
> Terra Incognita, attacked at night by treacherous natives
> were murdered at Boola Boola near La Grange Bay
> on the 13th November 1864
> Also as an appreciative token of remembrance of
> MAITLAND BROWN
> one of the pioneer pastoralists and premier politicians
> of this State, intrepid leader of the government search
> and punitive party, his remains together with the sad
> relics of the ill fated three recovered at great danger
> from the lone wilds repose under public monument in the
> East Perth Cemetery
> 'LEST WE FORGET'

Staff and students of Murdoch University objected to the plaque, conducted extensive research and gained the support of Aboriginal communities. After long negotiations with the Fremantle City Council it was agreed that a new plaque would be attached to the existing monument putting a different point of view. Its wording was:

> This plaque was erected by people
> who found the monument before you offensive.
> The monument describes the events at La Grange
> from one perspective only;
> the viewpoint of the white 'settlers'.
> No mention is made of the right of Aboriginal people
> to defend their land or of the history of provocation
> which led to the explorers' deaths.
> The 'punitive party' mentioned here ended in the
> deaths of somewhere around twenty Aboriginal people.
> The whites were well-armed and equipped and
> none of their party was killed or wounded.
> This plaque is in memory of the Aboriginal people
> killed at La Grange. It also commemorates all other
> Aboriginal people who died during the invasion of their country.

The Victorian Tourist Commission decided in 1989 to mark significant Aboriginal massacre sites in western Victoria. Considerable research was carried out identifying such locations over the next two years, but with the closure of the Koori Tourism Unit in 1991 the project was abandoned. The research by Ian Clark was eventually published as *Scars in the Landscape* by the Australian Institute of Aboriginal and Torres Strait Islander

Studies in 1995. But the desire to commemorate massacres and those killed in frontier conflict remains strong. In October 1998 prominent church leaders joined members of the Nimulla clan of the Kamilaroi people at the site of the Myall Creek massacre of 1838. Church people from all over Australia brought stones to the site to build a temporary cairn, 'hoping that eventually there [would] be a permanent memorial'. A month later a ceremony was held on the hill above the War Memorial in Canberra at the site of a plaque commemorating Aboriginal involvement in Australia's overseas wars, to pay silent tribute to 'the unknown thousands' of indigenous Australians who died in the only war to have been fought on the Australian continent, 'the war of white against black'.

The difficulty which Australia has experienced in deciding what to do about massacre sites is an indication of a more general problem – how to incorporate the 'border wars' into the central national story. Given their duration, geographical spread and numbers killed they would have to be considered alongside the two world wars rather than the smaller conflicts in the Sudan, South Africa, Korea and Vietnam. The issues at stake – the acquisition of continental sovereignty and control of the most productive lands in the country – were as momentous as those for which our soldiers died in the two world wars. Without a successful prosecution of the border wars there would not have been an Australian nation in any recognisable sense.

But domestic conflict presents other challenges. In relation to Australia's overseas wars it has been possible to avoid any sense of moral responsibility for either outbreak or outcome. We fought in wars declared and prosecuted by others according to geopolitical strategy over which we had little control. We could fight without having to take responsibility for the politics or the legality or the morality of the campaigns. We just did what we were asked to do.

Australians rarely appear to concern themselves with the obvious fact that at Gallipoli we assisted in the invasion of a country about which we knew little, with which we had almost no contact, which had never presented any threat to Australia, and in the process killed thousands of young Turkish men who were legitimately defending their homeland. We commemorate the event in the manner of innocents. It was the occasion for personal heroism, noble sacrifice and collective pride.

We cannot escape responsibility for the killing times. Before 1856 in eastern Australia and 1890 in the west, Britain shared culpability for the great tragedy and loss of life. After those dates we were on our own. We insisted that relations between colonists and indigenous people were an internal matter. We rejected interest or criticism from outside as unacceptable meddling in our affairs. But we find it hard to know how to respond to the destruction of Aboriginal society. It is surely a strange paradox that we can celebrate our failed assault on Turkey but feel embarrassed about the successful invasion of Australia. We have no difficulty about the fact that our young men died fighting for control of territory in France and Belgium, but we have problems in accepting that settlers fought to establish British authority over Australia. We like to think the continent just fell into our laps and shun the obvious fact that we killed and destroyed to acquire it. We are much more comfortable as innocent underdogs than as calculating overlords. For all their faults, one has to admire the brutal honesty of the frontiersmen who refused to disguise what they were doing and were willing to accept moral responsibility for their actions, seeing them as the necessary and logical consequence of colonisation, who were sharply aware of the 'terrible necessities' forced on them by their situation.

But in the nineteenth century there was not merely a reluctance to commemorate incidents of the border wars but a far wider refusal to do anything to perpetuate any memory at all of the prior owners of the country. Soon after the death of Truganini in Hobart in 1876, the historian James Calder wrote to the colonial Premier suggesting that the government raise a memorial in her honour. But the proposal was rejected, the Premier explaining that he was not persuaded by Calder's case and that while the government had been justified in providing liberally for Truganini's support 'while in life' it was questionable 'how far they should be warranted in devoting public funds to perpetuate her memory'.

A similar story was told by James Dawson, the pioneer ethnographer from the Western District of Victoria. In 1884 while he was away in the United Kingdom his friend, the Aboriginal elder Wombeetch Puyuun or Camperdown George, died and was buried in an unmarked grave outside the boundaries of the cemetery with no mark of respect; 'as if a black man was a brute', Dawson noted. He decided to erect a monument in the local cemetery and gained the permission of the trustees of the cemetery to exhume the body and re-bury it. At his own expense he erected a twenty-foot obelisk with the inscription:

In Memory of the Aborigines of this district.

He wrote to leading landowners seeking their support but received very little. In refusing to assist, the landowners remarked:

> I decline to assist in erecting a monument to a race of men we have robbed of their country.

> I have always looked on the blacks as a nuisance and hope the trustees will forbid its erection.

> Fail to see the use. The obelisk will point for all time to come to our treatment of this unfortunate race – the possessors of the soil we took from them, and we gave in return the vices belonging to our boasted civilization. I decline to assist.

The problem with memorials of any kind was that they reminded the colonists that the land had once belonged to the Aborigines and continued to point to that central moral issue 'for all time to come'. Any recounting of stories of conflict and bloodshed was problematic for the same reason. It raised the questions of what the fighting was all about, what its objectives were, its political purpose and what it achieved. And it didn't take too much investigation to come up with the same answer – the border wars were about the ownership and control of land, about taking it by force from those who had been in possession since time immemorial. And that is the principal reason why white Australians have always wanted to avoid all mention of warfare, because once discussion began it always had to lead back to the central issue of dispossession. A perceptive visitor to the Australian colonies in the 1840s noticed that 'the right to the country' was a 'sore subject' among the settlers, who strove to 'satisfy their consciences in various ways'. Such people found it difficult to look clearly and honestly at their past or to deal fairly with those they had wronged. They deferred dealing with these great problems and in so doing bequeathed them to their descendants.

XIII

Mabo and Land Rights

I don't think I had ever heard of Aboriginal land rights before I went to North Queensland in 1965. I'm sure I knew that there were large Aboriginal reserves in central Australia and Arnhem Land, but that was about as far as it went. The question was taken up during the Inter-Racial Seminar in December 1967. Faith Bandler referred to international interest in indigenous land rights and mentioned the recently adopted International Labour Organisation Convention 107, which urged countries to recognise the right of ownership 'collective or individual of members of the populations concerned over the lands traditionally occupied'. Faith commended the South Australian legislation which had been adopted a short time before, giving control of Aboriginal land to a Lands Trust dominated by indigenous members. One of the recommendations passed at the end of the seminar urged the Queensland government to follow South Australia's example and grant Aborigines title to the existing reserves and missions.

I no doubt voted for the motion and considered it a good thing but I don't think the question particularly engaged my interest, which was more closely focused on issues like education, housing and employment. Even more pressing at the time were the remaining authoritarian powers of the Department of Native Affairs, exercised both on settlements like Palm Island and also over anyone who was 'under the Act'.

I'm not sure now what I said in my Australian history lectures about land ownership. Not much, I suspect. I'm sure I never really questioned the current legal orthodoxy that Australia was what later came to be called a terra nullius. I had never heard the term at the time. I certainly thought it unjust and immoral that the Aborigines lost their country. But I assumed that nomadic people could have no claim on the land. That was certainly the impression that was conveyed by the books I had read. More commonly the issue wasn't discussed at all. The matter was settled and uncontroversial. In one of the standard texts of the time, *International Law*, D.P. O'Connell, Professor of Law at Adelaide University, declared that Australia had been legitimately treated as terra nullius because the Aborigines were 'held incapable of intelligent transactions with respect to land'. O'Connell questioned neither the judgement nor the reasons for it. I reflected on this situation when writing the preface to my book *The Law of the Land* in 1986:

> There was little disagreement from any point of the political or intellectual spectrum. Discovery, it was generally agreed, had delivered to the Europeans not just sovereignty over Australia but ownership of every inch of land as well; Australia was a colony of settlement not conquest; there had never been any recognition of native title; what ameliorative

measures were taken did not imply any acceptance of Aboriginal land rights.

I still look back and wonder at both how little I understood about the subject and the misplaced certainty I felt about what I did know. I can't remember what reaction I had to the decision in 1971 of Mr Justice Blackburn of the Northern Territory Supreme Court in the so-called Gove land rights case (or *Milerrpum v. Nabalco*). I suppose I must have read about it at the time in the papers. I certainly didn't read the case itself until years later. The Aborigines lost the case, with Blackburn deciding that there had never been any recognition of customary property rights in Australian courts and that the doctrine of terra nullius still ran in Australia. I probably thought the judgement was what was to be expected.

My thinking about land rights changed rapidly during 1972. I watched with great interest the Aboriginal campaign for land rights which followed the Gove land rights judgement and which culminated in the tent embassy on the lawns in front of Parliament House. At much the same time I had many long conversations with Eddie Mabo, who had come to the university to work as a groundsman. He used to come up to my room a couple of times a week and we would eat sandwiches, drink tea and talk. Sometimes it was just the two of us; sometimes Noel Loos joined us. We discussed many things, including our oral history project. But what interested me most was to hear Eddie's stories about growing up on Murray Island. He had a good memory and was a wonderful storyteller, and taught both Noel and me many things about life in a traditional community. He was also an intellectual in the precise sense of the word, despite having only a limited

European education. He was intensely interested in ideas, in culture and in anthropology. Eddie was also a Murray Island patriot who loved his homeland although he had not been back there for ten years. He would often talk about his village and about his own land, which he assured us would always be there when he returned because everyone knew it belonged to his family. His face shone when he talked of his village and his land.

So intense and so obvious was his attachment to his land that I began to worry about whether he had any idea at all about his legal circumstances. I was concerned about this for a couple of weeks and talked to Noel Loos about whether we should tell Eddie what the situation was. I think we probably worried about it for a couple of days after our conversation and decided that we had to warn him about the way things were. At our next lunch I cautiously broached the subject. I said something like: 'You know how you've been telling us about your land and how everyone knows it's Mabo land? Don't you realise that nobody actually owns land on Murray Island? It's all crown land.'

He was stunned. It was as though I had punched him in the face. He looked angry, aghast, incredulous. How could the whitefellas question something so obvious as his ownership of his land? And yet he trusted Noel and me and he knew that what I was saying was probably the truth. No doubt Eddie would have found this out himself sooner or later or someone else would have told him. But it was there over the sandwiches and tea that the first step was taken which led to the Mabo judgement in June 1992.

We discussed the situation again over the next few weeks. I remembered from my undergraduate American history that there had been a number of important Supreme Court cases in the 1820s and 1830s which established that the Indians had a form of land tenure known as Indian or native title. I checked this with my head of department, Brian Dalton, who taught American history, and he confirmed that it was indeed so. I think he actually gave me one of the judgements of the Chief Justice, John Marshall, to read.

By the next time I saw Eddie I was bursting to tell him about the American precedents. I said I thought he would have a very good case to take before the courts – easy enough to say, but I actually understood very little about the law. I knew enough about Murray Island to realise that it had an entirely different social structure, system of land use and tenure and different settlement patterns from those of the Aborigines on mainland Australia. The Murray Islanders were closely related to the Papuans; they were gardeners who lived in villages. Property was owned by families and not collectively. The small garden plots were clearly marked with boundaries which were known and normally recognised throughout the community.

I was still working on the assumption that the Aborigines could not be regarded as owners in Australian law because they were nomadic, had no permanent settlements and didn't work the land, or 'mix their labour with the soil' as John Locke, the seventeenth-century political philosopher, phrased it. I still accepted the doctrine of terra nullius but I had concluded that it shouldn't apply to Murray Island. I explained all this to Eddie with great enthusiasm, saying that he would have a good chance to succeed whereas Aborigines were bound to fail before the courts. We talked about taking a case to court on a number of other occasions. I said to him one day almost in jest that when he had won his court case he would be famous.

A few months later I was associated with what was probably

Eddie's second step along the road to the High Court. We decided that he should go back to Murray Island as my research assistant to record oral history. It suited him to do so because he could get leave from his job and my research grant would pay his fare. It took considerable negotiating before the university would allow him to be officially appointed as a part-time research assistant, because the regulations specified that such a person should have a degree. That difficulty was overcome and Eddie set off with a new tape recorder and a bag full of tapes. When he arrived on Thursday Island he was refused permission to land on any of the islands in the strait. The DNA administrators and the Island councils were adamant. Mabo was a troublemaker and a suspected communist and he was not wanted. Eddie flew back quite devastated. He was an exile who could not return to his own island. In a short space of time he had discovered that he had no legal right to his own land or to return to his village or to visit his relatives.

The critical moment in the journey to the High Court came some years later. In August 1981 the University Students Union and the Townsville Treaty Committee held a conference on the question of 'Land Rights and the Future of Australian Race Relations'. By then the debate about land rights had moved on. Conference convenors emphasised that they had no intention of organising a debate on whether land rights should be conceded. They took that for granted. What they wanted was a thorough discussion of all strategies which could 'conceivably lead to the full and uncompromising implementation of land rights throughout Australia'. In the subsequent discussion a number of potential strategies were discussed, including 'international pressure and the possibility of bringing about a definitive High Court decision on the question'.

The conference brought to Townsville a number of lawyers familiar with questions of indigenous rights in both domestic and international law. Barbara Hocking and Greg McIntyre gave papers canvassing the possibility of taking a land rights case to the High Court, referring to both British and North American jurisprudence. Eddie Mabo and his fellow Murray Islanders were able for the first time to talk to people who knew exactly what to do to mount a challenge to traditional legal doctrine. The lawyers met the indigenous people, who had a powerful desire to claim their rights in court and who presented them with circumstances that were more likely to succeed than any other possible case in Australia.

I had little to do with the case itself from that time, beyond asking Eddie whenever I saw him how it was progressing during its tortuous eleven-year course through the courts. I happened to be in Canberra in May 1991 when final submissions were heard in *Mabo v. Queensland*, No. 2. My son, John, and I met Eddie quite by chance outside the court and we sat together through the proceedings, which were formal and not particularly interesting. But one exchange dramatised the fundamental issue at stake, which was who owned the land on the Murray Island group – the people who lived there or the Queensland government? The Solicitor-General of Queensland was giving his final submission. Justice Mary Gaudron questioned him. She asked whether his position was that from the time when the Islands were annexed in 1879 the Islanders were trespassers on crown land who at any moment could, legally, have been driven into the sea. The Solicitor-General looked uncomfortable but said that he guessed that was indeed the Queensland position.

Afterwards we reminisced about how much had happened in

the almost twenty years since we used to discuss questions of law and justice over our sandwiches. He was confident that he would win the case. I was less sure. But I was amazed at the fortitude and determination he had shown during all the twists and turns of the legal process. He was consumed by his mission to gain the recognition that Murray Islanders owned their land. He wanted Australian society to recognise and respect both their ownership and their culture. But the second part of the equation was that he believed in the Australian legal system and continued to do so through all his tribulations. He was convinced that if he could explain the Islanders' relationship with the land, their love of their islands, the nature of traditional ownership, tenure and inheritance then the courts would understand. It was a profound vote of confidence in Australian law and Australian society. Many other indigenous Australians thought he was deluded in his confidence in whitefella justice. Many white Australians were convinced that when shove came to push the courts would side with the big end of town and that he was bound to lose.

John and I farewelled Eddie at the end of the afternoon. He was getting the bus back to Townsville – a long and arduous journey. I didn't see him again. But I had a vivid dream about him later when I was in Canada, just before his death. I was standing somewhere out-of-doors. I saw Eddie coming towards me. He was surrounded by some sort of glowing light; silver and phosphorescent. We met and shook hands. I put my left hand on his shoulder and said that the case would soon be decided and that I was sure he shouldn't worry about 'this other matter' (his sickness) because I was certain he would soon get over it. I don't think he said anything in reply. But he began to move away. He was gliding rather than walking. Our hands came apart. We were both crying.

It was an intense and powerful dream. It assumed even more significance when we heard news of his death from Australia a day or two later. One of the few people I told about it was Eddie's nephew, Bill Lowah. I said how perplexing and disturbing it had been. Bill laughed loudly and said that of course Eddie had come to visit me before he died. It seemed so natural to Bill – the most normal thing in the world. To me it was an awesome occurrence, shaking the solid rock of reason on which I like to stand.

With the Mabo case before the courts I realised how little I knew about the law and the many legal issues which underlay the whole colonial venture. As teaching and other commitments allowed I set out to remedy the situation and in the process came to realise how poorly equipped I had been to deal with questions which were central to my main research project – the relations between settlers and indigenous Australians. I felt embarrassed that I had taught these issues so badly and lectured confidently in areas where I was, at best, ill informed. There were so many things I had taken for granted and which should have been questioned. As with my earlier studies of frontier history I felt I should have known better; I should have been told somewhere in my education about all those questions which suddenly confronted Australia with the emergence of the Aboriginal land rights movement. When I came to write about these issues, as I did in *The Law of the Land*, there was a sharpness of tone, a sense of exasperation, an urgency to put things right that were as much to do with what I thought had been my own failings as with those of Australian society as a whole.

I had assumed all along that, while morality was on the side of the indigenes, law was securely in the camp of the colonists and that the camp itself was well defended and probably impregnable. That was the reason why I wasn't surprised or shocked when, in 1971, Mr Justice Blackburn declared that the Yolngu people of Yirrakala did not own their land. That, I thought, was the logic of the law. The concurrence with orthodoxy led me to accept without question the idea that the British claim over eastern Australia in 1770 was a legitimate one, unproblematic in European international law; that the annexation of 1788 delivered to the British both sovereignty over half the continent and beneficial ownership of the land. I assumed that the Aborigines were accorded no right to land because they were nomadic and that the common law always sided with those who made better use of the soil. I thought Australia stood out internationally in the matter of native title because the Aborigines were thought by the settlers to be uniquely primitive and that their treatment of Australia as terra nullius followed logically from that assumption. Which was why I thought the Murray Islanders would stand a good chance of proving that they actually owned their land.

My confident assumptions about settlement and law were rapidly undermined as I read widely in both the history of international law and the jurisprudence of other common-law settler societies – New Zealand, Canada and the United States. The nature and consequences of discovery suddenly seemed much more problematic than they had been before. Captain James Cook did indeed sail right along the east coast of Australia, was probably the first European to do so, and claimed eastern Australia for the British crown when he landed on Possession Island in Torres Strait. I think that, like most Australians of my generation, I had grown up with the idea that Cook's skill and

fortitude had 'earned' the continent for Britain. But such a claim
was an 'outward'-looking rather than an 'inward'-looking one. It
was directed at other European powers to establish an exclusive
sphere of influence. It meant very little as far as the Aborigines
were concerned. I found this a most surprising idea, one that I
had never come across before. The law in question was clearly
stated by Chief Justice Marshall in the American Supreme Court
in 1832, when he explained that claims of discovery 'asserted a
title against Europeans only and were considered as blank pages
so far as the right of the natives were concerned'. There were
even more unsettling questions about the concept of discovery in
international law which raised the issue of whether it could apply
at all to occupied territory. The great seventeenth-century Dutch
jurist Hugo Grotius argued that it was 'shameless' to:

> claim for oneself by right of discovery what is held by
> another, even though the occupant may be wicked, may hold
> wrong views about God, or may be dull of wit. For discovery
> applies to those things which belong to no one.

Another issue about the British claims of 1770 and 1788 was
that they covered far too large an area to be valid. The small
settlement at Sydney Cove was quite insufficient to sustain a
claim over half a continent for, as an eighteenth-century jurist
remarked, an individual or a nation who only 'seized a thing with
his eyes, but does not take hold of it, cannot be said to occupy'.
The dubious nature of Britain's expansive claim to sovereignty
was discussed in 1966 by the leading authority on imperial and
Commonwealth law, Sir Kenneth Roberts Wray. In his book
Commonwealth and Colonial Law he argued that the traditional

Australian view of the first settlement was 'startling' and 'incredible'. He greatly doubted whether:

> a foothold in a small area of the east side of a sub-continent 2000 miles wide [would] be sufficient in English law (as it certainly would not be in international law) to confer sovereignty but also title to the soil throughout the hinterland of nearly three million square miles.

I had never come across anything in Australian history books which cast any doubt on the effectiveness of Cook's and Phillip's claims of sovereignty. They were holy writ which never seemed to be questioned.

The question of Aboriginal land ownership also became much more complex. I came to the conclusion that international law of the late eighteenth century recognised that itinerant pastoralists or hunter/gatherers were actually in occupation of their land and had a form of title which could be encompassed within existing European legal codes. As with the doctrine of discovery, the whole question was thrashed out in the American courts in the 1820s and 1830s. Chief Justice Marshall declared in 1832 that Indian native title did not depend on the particular use they made of the land:

> Hunting was at that time the principal occupation of the Indians, and their land was more used for that purpose than for any other; . . . To the United States it could be a matter of no concern, whether their whole territory was devoted to hunting grounds, or whether an occasional village or an occasional cornfield interrupted and gave some variety to the scene.

Marshall's summary of the principles of native title has always been regarded as a classic statement of both common and international law as it was understood in the late eighteenth century and early nineteenth century.

But the question still remained. Why did the British act as though the Aborigines did not own the land? Why didn't they make provision for treaties or authorised purchase of land? I came to the conclusion that it was not so much a matter of thinking the Aborigines uniquely primitive but rather the belief that Australia itself was largely uninhabited and, therefore, literally a terra nullius. This was the advice given to the imperial government by Sir Joseph Banks, the acknowledged expert on the matter and a man of authority and influence. The behaviour of the officers of the First Fleet bore out this interpretation. They acted as though they expected all but the coastal fringe to be empty and were obviously surprised when they discovered Aborigines living permanently away from the ocean. This interpretation is still controversial. But in my view it explains what happened and it hasn't been effectively rebutted by contradictory evidence. So terra nullius resulted not from primitive Aborigines but from erring Europeans.

If my hunch was right, the British would likely have realised their mistake and changed their mind about Aboriginal property rights. But were there documents to indicate they did? I set out to find them. From the start of my research I came across scraps of evidence which suggested British officials in both Australia and Britain had indeed concluded that Aborigines were in possession of their land. Governor King advised his successor, Governor Bligh, in 1807 that he had 'ever considered the natives the real proprietors of the soil'. Many colonists also came to this conclusion during the first fifty years of settlement and said so in speeches, books and letters. In London, the Colonial Office officials responded to the weight of evidence that was arriving from Australia. The Permanent Head of the Department, James Stephen, wrote a memo to his Minister in 1840 on a despatch that had come in from South Australia: 'It is an important and unsuspected fact that these Tribes had Proprietary [*sic*] in the Soil, that is, in particular sections of it which were clearly defined and well understood before the occupation of their country.'

I had quite early in my research come to the conclusion that the British authorities had decided that Australia was not a special case, that whatever had happened at the first settlement, the Aborigines did have a form of tenure; that is, they held native title over Australia. This did not mean that colonisation should cease. Rather it was a matter of either purchasing land directly from the traditional owners or compensating them in other ways for land expropriated without negotiation. This was a controversial proposition. If true, it could dramatically change the interpretation of both colonial history and jurisprudence. Although there was much circumstantial evidence, for a long time I couldn't come across anything that was sufficient to clinch the argument.

It turned up unexpectedly on an afternoon of research that had provided little that was useful. I had spent several hours reading microfilmed copies of handwritten Colonial Office records from the 1830s. Using microfilm is an arduous business at any time – trying to read quickly faded or indecipherable handwriting, much of it not relevant to the task in hand. But you never know what might turn up, so you stick at it until your head spins and your eyes blur. I had scarcely taken a note during a couple of hours of fruitless reading and was about to give up and rewind the film. Suddenly, and unexpectedly, I came across the minute books of the South Australian Colonization Commission, the private entrepreneurial organisation that was promoting the new settlement. The minutes related to meetings held just before the departure of the first settlers in 1836 and covered the period when the Commission Chairman, Robert Torrens, was negotiating with the Colonial Office to receive final approval for the venture.

The minutes were hard to read. They had been written with a very thick pen and the paper had absorbed too much ink. At first sight they seemed to be fairly routine and not particularly useful. I glanced quickly at them and moved the film on. Suddenly I saw an entry that totally startled me. It was an account of a recent meeting between Torrens and the Secretary of State for the Colonies, Lord Glenelg, who had told Torrens that the Commissioners 'were to prepare a plan for securing the rights of the Aborigines which plan should include the appointment of a Colonial Officer to be called Protector of Aborigines and arrangements for purchasing the lands of the Natives'.

I re-read the sentence, made sure I had got it right, turned the machine off, left the library and went for a walk. It was what I had been looking for, what I had thought should be there somewhere in the records. It was like discovering a nugget of gold. Here was the confirmation that in the centre of Empire there was no longer any sense of terra nullius. The Aborigines were landowners. What was in contention was 'the lands of the Natives'. The tenure was secure enough to be recognised in law – the natives had rights which were to be protected. The colonists were required to purchase the land. Short of any specific

199

statement at a later date confirming the doctrine of terra nullius, we can conclude that by 1836 it had been abandoned in the Colonial Office.

As it turned out, the South Australian Colonization Commission deliberately and successfully evaded its clear commitment to purchase Aboriginal land. But for the next twenty years British policy was shaped by a recognised responsibility to provide compensation for Aboriginal land – for an 'equivalence' as it was called at the time. There were three major relevant initiatives: establishment of reserves, the commitment of funds from land sales to pay for education and health services, and the creation of a form of land tenure which allowed Aborigines and pastoralists to share the same land. The instrument was called the pastoral lease, of which more will be said later.

Even after all my research and dramatic change of mind about native title, I was not all that confident that the Islanders would be victorious in the High Court despite what I thought was the legal strength of their case. I was delighted when the news of the 6–1 judgement came through. But like so many other people, I felt that the victory was shadowed by Eddie Mabo's death earlier in the year. If only he could have lived to know he had won. How delighted he would have been! How vindicated he would have felt! His name was to be forever linked with one of the most important legal decisions in Australian history, a real turning point after which nothing could ever be the same again. We had joked about Mabo becoming a famous name. We never imagined things would turn out in the way they did.

While I had not been confident about the result, I was certain that both Court and judgement would come in for intense criticism. It took longer to emerge than I expected and was, to my surprise, more about history than law. The Court, it was asserted, had got its history wrong, and that had clouded the bench's legal judgement. Critics like Professor Geoffrey Blainey argued that the judges had imposed contemporary views and standards on the late eighteenth century and early nineteenth century. They applied 'supposedly dominant moral values' of the 1990s back to 1788 and reversed the legal thinking 'of long ago'. The problem with this argument was that the Court, in recognising native title in Australia, picked up the legal principles which had governed the transactions of settlers and indigenous people in North America since the eighteenth century. The judges applied old principles to a contemporary legal problem. The jurisprudential traffic was from past to present, not the other way around. The Court brought Australia into line with comparable common-law countries. The only surprising feature of the whole matter was that it had taken local courts so long to do so.

The moral issues involved were not new either. They were not the recent product of rampant political correctness. Indeed they had been debated and agonised over since the very beginning of European settlement. I had been continually struck by the intensity of the colonial debate about the morality of settlement, about the legitimacy of expropriation of Aboriginal land, about the need for the payment of compensation. The Tasmanian 'Aboriginal Protector', George Augustus Robinson, captured the character of the debate when in 1832 he remarked, 'I am at a loss to conceive by what tenure we hold this country, for it does not appear to be that we either hold it by conquest or by right of purchase'. Another related argument – that Australia had been treated differently from North America or New Zealand because the Aborigines were nomadic hunters and gatherers – had little to sustain it. Throughout the eighteenth and nineteenth century legal orthodoxies confirmed the principle that hunters were as much in possession as pastoralists or farmers, as the Marshall judgements established. A famous House of Commons Select Committee report of 1836–37 on the native peoples of the Empire concluded that: 'It might be presumed that the native inhabitants of any land have an incontrovertible right to their own soil'. The assumptions made there were very similar to those of Chief Justice Brennan in the Mabo case when he argued that: 'The ownership of land in the exclusive occupation of a people must be vested in that people: land is susceptible of ownership and there are no other owners'.

The influence of the new historical writing on the High Court remains a contentious issue. But there can be no doubt that the Mabo judgement has changed the way the story of Australian colonisation must in future be told. Before Mabo the story began with the Crown exercising sovereignty and holding the beneficial ownership of all the land in eastern Australia, with the same process unfolding in central Australia in 1824 and western Australia in 1829. Therefore, when colonists pushed into the interior they travelled through and settled on vacant crown land. They had as good a right to be there as the resident Aborigines, and once they had settled, a better right, which allowed them to defend their property against indigenous incursion.

The new post-Mabo story is quite different. It begins with the Crown claiming sovereignty over the continent and beneficial ownership of only the tiny areas actually occupied. The continent as a whole was in the possession of the indigenous nations, whose native title was recognised by the common law. Indigenous ownership was extinguished in a piecemeal fashion over many years; but much of the exploration and pioneer settlement was conducted by Europeans trespassing on indigenous land, in many cases expropriating the legitimate owners by force. Aboriginal resistance to this process was in a strictly legal sense a justifiable defence of their rights. Where extinguishment of indigenous property rights could not be proven, as on Murray Island, it must be assumed that native title may have survived. But whether extinguishment has occurred or not, indigenous communities either currently own land under native title or have done so in the past and have a moral, if not a legal, right to compensation. This places them in a very different situation from the one they experienced when terra nullius was the pervading doctrine. They either were once or are still landowners, with the respect that position brings and all the legal protection provided by the common law famous for its defence of private property.

With Mabo, suddenly many Aboriginal communities had gained something to bring to the negotiating table of national life. The fringe dwellers had become property owners, and the implications of their new circumstances became apparent in a dramatic way in the Wik judgement of December 1996.

XIV

Wik, Pastoral Leases and the Pursuit of Justice

The High Court handed down its decision in the Wik case late on Friday morning a week before Christmas in 1996. Margaret and I were in Launceston at the time. We were having lunch and I hurried out of the restaurant just before one o'clock to hear the radio news. The car was standing beside a park dating back to the early colonial period, in the dense shade cast by an avenue of large oak trees. It was like a small imported piece of England. It would be hard to imagine any part of Australia further removed in space and spirit from the vast sun-drenched savannah which was in contention in the Court.

I was both delighted and surprised with the news that the bench had decided by a 4–3 majority that pastoral leases did not necessarily extinguish native title. Delighted because I had been involved in the case for several years as a consultant for the Cape York Land Council and because I had argued along the lines of the majority judgement over several years, often in the face of dismissal and disbelief from professional lawyers, politicians and government advisers. Surprised because, regardless of my own views about the relevant laws, I was convinced that the case would be lost, that at best it would go down 3–4.

In talking about Wik around the country I found that the common view was that it was very complex and hard to understand. This was not really the case. There were two main contenders – the Wik and Thayorre peoples of western Cape York on the one hand and the Queensland government on the other. There were two areas of land in question – the so-called Holroyd lease of 2800 square kilometres, and the Mitchelton leases which were just under half that size. Both had at some stage been held under pastoral lease – the Mitchelton leases between 1910 and 1922 and the Holroyd lease from 1945 to the present. The Mitchelton country was never occupied and in 1922 was absorbed into a nearby Aboriginal reserve. The Holroyd lease had never been fenced or undergone significant development. The Wik and Thayorre people continued to live on their traditional lands, which, they asserted, embraced the two large pastoral leases.

So the matter in contention was whether the issuing of a pastoral lease extinguished for all time the pre-existing native title of the traditional land-holders. The case as presented by Queensland, the Commonwealth and other state governments was that settled common-law doctrine determined that a lease gave the lessee an exclusive right of possession for the term of the lease, which would as a matter of course extinguish all surviving native title rights. Lawyers for the Wik and Thayorre peoples argued to the contrary that a pastoral lease could not be seen as a traditional common-law lease. It was a unique form of land tenure which grew out of specific geographical conditions and historical circumstances and had to be considered in that light. Pastoral leases clearly limited the rights of the lessee to those activities associated with pastoral pursuits and so could not be seen as extinguishing native title.

While agreeing with counsel for the Aborigines, Mr Justice Kirby observed:

> Their argument was simple and correct. Pastoral leases give rise to statutory interests in land which are sui generis. Being creatures of Australian statutes, their character and incidents must be derived from the statute. Neither of the Acts [Queensland Land Acts, 1910, 1962] in question here expressly extinguishes native title. To do so very clear statutory language would, by conventional theory, be required. When the Acts are examined, clear language of extinguishment is simply missing. On the contrary, there are several indications which support the contention of the Wik and the Thayorre that the interest in land which was granted to the pastoralist was a limited one: for 'grazing purposes only', as the leases stated. Such an interest could, in law, be exercised and enjoyed to the full without necessarily extinguishing native title interests. The extent to which the two interests could operate together is a matter for further evidence and legal analysis. Only if there is inconsistency between the legal interests of the lessee (as defined by the instrument of lease and the legislation under which it is granted) and the native title (as established by evidence), will such native title, to the extent of inconsistency, be extinguished.

My involvement with the case concerned the history of pastoral leases which were created by Colonial Office officials in Britain in the middle of the nineteenth century. A detailed study written and researched in partnership with a solicitor for the Cape York Land Council, Jamie Dalziel, was presented to the Court. It grew out of my earlier work on British attitudes to native title and turned on the assumption that the imperial authorities had given up the proposition that Australia was a terra nullius, that they believed that the Aborigines had rights to their traditional lands and when those rights were extinguished there was a requirement to provide for compensation in some form, or an equivalence as it was often called. But these assumptions had been dramatically challenged in the 1830s by the vast illegal occupation of land throughout south-eastern Australia known as the squatting rush. For British policy makers it was both unexpected and unprecedented.

Officials in both Sydney and London knew that they lacked the power or the means to bring the squatters and their flocks and herds back within the settled districts. It was a problem which the Permanent Head of the Colonial Office, James Stephen, concluded was 'admitting of none but a very imperfect solution'. It was obvious that the future of New South Wales was dependent on the wool industry and that the flocks needed 'a free range over the wide expanse of herbage', as Governor Bourke phrased it. But the squatting rush created almost impossible conditions for governments seeking to retain some control over the activities of the settlers, 'persons hanging on the Frontiers of a vast pastoral country to which there is no known assignable limit'. James Stephen thought the 'shepherds and herdsmen of New South Wales' would become like the nomadic tribes of central Asia and would be 'almost as lawless and migratory a Race'.

Two other concerns weighed heavily on the minds of colonial officials. They feared that the squatters would ultimately gain control of the lands they occupied and claim freehold rights either on the basis of prescription or by applying pressure to future local parliaments. In that way the vast interior would be locked up in the control of a few hundred individuals who had been first on the scene. There was deep concern, also, about the fate of the Aborigines. The Colonial Office officials read regular dispatches from all the Australian colonies. They were keenly aware of, and deeply disturbed by, the continual violence on the frontiers of settlement. In their internal memos they expressed their fear that the settlers would annihilate the tribes. This would be a 'calamity', a 'catastrophe' which would deeply stain the honour of the British government. Governor Gipps reflected humanitarian concern in Britain, and in an official announcement in 1839 emphasised:

> the importance which Her Majesty's Government, and no
> less the Parliament and the people of Great Britain attach to
> the just and humane treatment of the Aborigines of this
> country; and to declare most earnestly, and solemnly, her
> deep conviction that there is no subject or matter whatsoever
> in which the interest as well as the honour of the Colonists
> are more essentially concerned.

The problem of how to protect the rights of the Aborigines on the vast pastoral frontier of south-eastern Australia intensified when in 1846 the imperial government agreed to give the pastoralists greater security of tenure on their runs. The extreme vulnerability of the Aboriginal position was commented on by the Protectors of Aborigines at Port Phillip, E.S. Parker and G.A. Robinson. Parker observed that unless reserves were set aside for the local clans, 'every acre of their native soil will shortly be so leased out and occupied as to leave them, in a legal view, no place for the soles of their feet'. Robinson begged the colonial and imperial governments to recognise the claim of the Aborigines 'to a reasonable share in the Soil of their fatherland'.

Robinson's and Parker's pleas were ignored in Sydney but in London they were noticed and acted upon. They had urged the creation of reserves, but Colonial Office officials concluded that they were not appropriate in Australia, given the nature of the country and the need for Aborigines to hunt and gather over large areas of land. The Secretary of State for the Colonies, Earl Grey, sent a dispatch to Sydney in February 1848 explaining that:

> the very difficulty of thus locating the Aboriginal Tribes absolutely apart from the Settlers renders it more incumbent on Government to prevent them from being altogether excluded from the land under pastoral occupation. I think it essential that it should be generally understood that leases granted for this purpose give the grantees only an exclusive right of pasturage for their cattle, and of cultivating such land as they may require within the large limits thus assigned to them, but that leases are not intended to deprive the natives of their former right to hunt over these Districts, or to wander over them in search of subsistence, in the manner to which they have been heretofore accustomed, from the

spontaneous produce of the soil except over land actually cultivated or fenced in for that purpose.

In a later memo Grey was even clearer about Aboriginal rights. He argued that it could be fairly assumed that the British government 'did not intend and had no power by these leases to exclude the natives from the use they had been accustomed to make of these unimproved lands'. In a subsequent dispatch sent to New South Wales in August 1849 Grey returned to the same principle, emphasising that there could be little doubt that the intention of the government was to give 'only the exclusive right of pasturage in the runs, not the exclusive occupation of the lands, as against natives using it for ordinary purposes'. The evidence, then, is very clear. The Colonial Office created pastoral leases to allow for the mutual use of the same land – the pastoralist had a right to conduct his pastoral enterprise, the Aborigines to use the land in their traditional manner. The pastoralist had no authority to deny access to the customary owners, who had rights which had to be respected. They were rights not granted by government but recognised to exist because they derived from the time before the arrival of the Europeans.

Eventually pastoral leases in New South Wales and subsequently in Queensland were provided, with a clause reserving to the Aboriginal inhabitants of the colony 'such free access to the said Run or Parcel of land . . . and to the trees and water thereon as will enable them to procure the Animals, Birds, Fish and other food on which they subsist'. Similar reservations were inserted in leases in Western Australia and South Australia. In Western Australia the wording was: 'Nothing contained in any pastoral lease shall prevent Aboriginal natives of this colony from entering upon the lands comprised therein, and seeking their subsistence therefrom in their accustomed manner'.

The South Australian reservation was much more detailed, guaranteeing to the Aboriginal inhabitants and their descendants:

> full and free rights of ingress, egress and regress into upon and over the said Waste Lands of the Crown . . . and every part thereof and in and to the springs and surface water thereon . . . and may at all times . . . use occupy dwell on and obtain food and water thereon and thereof . . . and may erect such wurlies and other dwellings as they have been heretofore accustomed to make and to take and use for food birds and animals . . . in such manner as they would have been entitled to if this demise had not been made.

This recognition of Aboriginal rights on pastoral land was clearly of major significance in the history of relations between settlers and indigenous people. It had received both the imprimatur of the imperial government and the personal endorsement of the Secretary of State, Earl Grey. The British officials believed that it was a matter of both high principle and practical necessity. Without a legally protected right to live on their own country, the Aboriginal clans would be exterminated. The honour of both Britain and Australia was at stake – but the Aboriginal right of residence and use was usually overridden by both settlers and colonial governments, and has largely been ignored in retrospect by the historians of land settlement.

An understanding of the terms of pastoral leases opens up new ways to see the history of pioneering after 1850. Those few settlers who negotiated local agreements with the resident clans were conforming to the conditions of their leases. Their fellows, who believed they 'should keep the blacks out' or that 'blacks and cattle don't mix' and acted accordingly, did so in direct contravention of the terms of the leases and should have forfeited them as a consequence of noncompliance. Right across north Australia there was a deliberate and massive evasion of a central aspect of the pastoral leases, aided and abetted by government. The Queensland authorities, in particular, discouraged the practice of 'letting in' the Aborigines which was a legal requirement of all lessees. The consequences for the Aborigines were discussed by the Protector of Aborigines in North Queensland, Dr Walter Roth, in 1903:

> Notwithstanding the efforts of myself and other Protectors to combat it, the assumption continues to prevail that because a large area of land is held from the Crown on lease, licence or other tenure, the lessee has the legal right to prevent aboriginals roaming or hunting over it; even living on it . . . the principle must be rigidly instilled that the aboriginal has as much a right to exist as the European, and certainly a greater right, not only to collect native fruits, but also to hunt and dispose of the game upon which they have vitally depended from time immemorial. Were the assumption just mentioned to be carried to its logical conclusion, and all available country leased or licensed, we should have a condition of affairs represented by a general starvation of all the aboriginals and their concurrent expulsion from the State.

The general colonial view was that the British officials sitting comfortably in Downing Street knew nothing about conditions

in Australia and were prone to sentimental and impractical policies which made little sense on the ground. But the assessment
they made in the 1840s that it was both necessary and possible for
Aborigines and pastoralists to share the same land proved to
be prescient. The mutual use they sought did not eventuate in
exactly the way they envisaged. But the classic pastoral system
which operated in many parts of Australia from the middle of the
nineteenth century to the 1960s was totally dependent on the use
of Aboriginal labour, and on Aborigines' ability to live in both the
traditional economy and the European one and move back and
forth between both.

What makes the Colonial Office's deliberations about
Australian land policy in the 1840s relevant today is that the
pastoral lease still bears the imprint of its creation. Pastoralists
generally continue to pay small annual fees for their leasehold
tenure but they are limited in what they can do on the land and
usually to activity directly related to the pastoral industry. Leases
are often 'for pastoral purposes only'. In Western Australia,
South Australia and the Northern Territory all leases still contain
reservations providing for Aboriginal use and access. Wording
has changed over the years, but the meaning and spirit remain as
they were in 1850. The leases have always contained such reservations, with the exception of a two-year hiatus in Western
Australia in the 1930s. The Northern Territory Crown Lands
Ordinance of 1978 provides for reservations in favour of the
Aborigines in the following manner:

> S.24/(2) . . . in any lease under this Ordinance a reservation
> in favour of the Aboriginal inhabitants of the Northern Terri-
> tory shall be read as a reservation permitting the Aboriginal

inhabitants of the leased land and the Aboriginal inhabitants of the Northern Territory who in accordance with Aboriginal tradition are entitled to inhabit the leased land —

(a) to enter and be on the leased land;

(b) to take and use the natural waters and springs on the leased land;

(c) subject to any other law in force in the Northern Territory, to take or kill for food or for ceremonial purposes animals ferae naturae on the leased land; and

(d) subject to any other law in force in the Northern Territory, to take for food or for ceremonial purposes any vegetable matter growing naturally on the leased land.

A clear line, therefore, can be drawn from the Colonial Office in 1848 to Australia in 1998, from the second Earl Grey to the four judges who formed the majority in the Wik case, whose decision came as such a surprise because the origins and history of pastoral leases had been forgotten. If this were merely a matter of overlooking obscure detail of land law it wouldn't matter so much. But the reservations protecting Aboriginal rights were much more significant. They did not create rights; they recognised their existence, their origin buried deep in time before the arrival of the first colonists. The British officials saw the recognition and protection of Aboriginal rights to continue to live on pastoral lands as essential to the survival of indigenous society; it was an obligation of profound importance which went right to the heart of the morality of the whole colonial venture. In 1850 Earl Grey wrote to the Governor of New South Wales, Sir Charles FitzRoy, observing that 'in assuming their territory the Settlers in Australia had incurred a moral obligation of the most sacred kind'. He thought that 'the honour of the local government is concerned in proving that no effort has been wanting on their part to avert the destruction of the Native Race as a consequence of the occupation of their territory by British subjects'. The continuing recognition of Aboriginal rights over the vast pastoral lands of the continent was, from the British point of view, the most important single test of honour for the Australian colonies.

The Queensland government began issuing leases without the reservation protecting Aboriginal rights some time early in the twentieth century, in circumstances which are still unknown. It may have been a purely administrative decision taken obscurely in the Lands Department. There was apparently no relevant debate or notice in the Parliament, no official statement in the *Government Gazette* or reference in legislation. But the absence of the reservation in twentieth-century leases led many observers and consultants to assume that native title had thereby been extinguished. The judges of the High Court decided otherwise, for two reasons. Given the existence of native title and its statutory protection on pastoral leases throughout the nineteenth century, it could only have been extinguished if the government had done so in a clear and plain manner. That was never done. The second issue concerned the nature of the pastoral lease itself. Its terms were so clear, precise and limited that it could not be assumed to have extinguished native title, which could survive even without a reservation in favour of the traditional owners. In that sense Queensland was no different from South Australia, Western Australia or the Northern Territory. The presumption was that where indigenous communities had maintained connection with their land they retained rights of use and access, although they had to be subordinated at all times to the pastoralist's right as specified in the lease document.

It is important to be clear where these rights came from. They were not created or invented by the High Court, neither were they the gift of government, be it federal, state, colonial or imperial. They were recognised as pre-existing rights by the Colonial Office and given statutory backing. They derived from Aboriginal society as it was before settlement. Native title is not new title; it is ancient title belatedly recognised. Those people who can establish use and access rights on pastoral leases are merely the present beneficiaries of land tenure which dates back hundreds of generations. In all likelihood it is the oldest continuing system of land tenure in the world.

While I was pleasantly surprised by the Wik decision, there were many others who were shocked and angered by it. This was partly because it was unexpected. There were many people who, like the Deputy Prime Minister, Tim Fischer, had pressed the Court to hand down its judgement in the expectation that it would put an end to Aboriginal ambitions in relation to pastoral lease land once and for all. Part of the problem was that so many legal firms had given bad advice to corporations and producer organisations. They had argued that a lease, by giving exclusive possession for the term in question, would extinguish native title, as the then Chief Justice, Sir Gerard Brennan, had suggested in the Mabo case in relation to two small leases on the Murray Islands.

Another cause of consternation was that Mabo and Wik dealt with two quite different sorts of land. In Mabo it was assumed that native title had potentially survived on vacant crown land,

those areas for which in 200 years the settlers had failed to find
an economic use. There was much of it, the area looked impressive or threatening on maps, but from the Europeans' point of
view it was largely useless country. Pastoral leases were quite different. They covered over 40 per cent of the land surface of the
continent and included some of the best grasslands in Australia,
although some of the land in question had always been marginally
productive or had become significantly degraded.

But there were other stakeholders apart from the Crown.
Some of the leaseholders had been on the land for many years
and had come to think of the land as theirs and of themselves as
landowners rather than as lessees of the Crown. This was especially true in Queensland, where it was confidently expected the
Wik case would be lost. Pastoralists there were dealt a double
blow. The High Court reminded them of the true, but almost
forgotten, nature of their tenure, and of their relationship with
the land they had come to see as theirs – that is, they had what in
effect was only a licence to conduct a pastoral enterprise. The
second blow was even more severe – the sudden and shocking
revelation that the local Aborigines in all likelihood were stakeholders in the land, with putative rights to enter and use it in par-
allel with the operations of the station. In one moment the status
of the pastoralist was depressed, that of the Aborigines elevated.
In the hierarchical, status-conscious world of rural Queensland
this was tantamount to revolution. The resulting anger and anxiety were scarcely surprising. The great pity was that they were
deliberately intensified by conservative politicians and producer
organisations in order to whip up a storm of protest which swept
through rural Australia.

Critics of the Wik decision gave the inescapable impression

that Aboriginal property rights lacked legitimacy. The Prime Minister, John Howard, declared soon after the judgement that the High Court had swung the pendulum too far towards the Aborigines and it was necessary to bring it back into equilibrium, by which he meant that rights recently recognised would have to be diminished by legislation. Dress that up as he might, it was clear that he was talking of expropriation of property rights in the interests of the pastoral leaseholders – or the owners, as he called them in his speech to graziers in Longreach. The Aborigines were never given the status of the other participants in the long and tortuous negotiation. They were not asked to a meeting of so-called stakeholders at the Lodge in Canberra which included the representatives of farming and mining industries, even though miners could at best be seen as potential stakeholders over much of the country in question. There was never any recognition in the Prime Minister's speeches that there was a long history to be considered or that leases in more than half the country had always contained reservations which protected native title rights.

The stand taken by National Party (NP) politicians and the National Farmers Federation (NFF) was even more extreme. Tim Fischer, the federal leader of the NP, boasted that there would be 'bucket-loads of extinguishment' in the government's legislative response to Wik. NP leaders in the states were even more hostile to the High Court's decision. But the most aggressive and uncompromising opposition came from the officials of the NFF, who were distinguished by the vehemence with which they demanded that the federal government expropriate Aboriginal property rights across vast tracts of the continent, including, it often seemed, even those embodied in the reservations in place since the middle of the nineteenth century. They spoke in the name of the pastoralists, among whom there appeared to be no collective memory of the debt owing to generations of Aboriginal workers whose unpaid labour had been the inescapable mainstay of the industry.

The intransigence of the Queensland NP and the NFF encouraged the One Nation party of Pauline Hanson to campaign for the complete expropriation of Aboriginal native title rights throughout the country. For if the Wik decision was as extreme and damaging as mainstream conservative politicians were insisting, why was Mabo not also unacceptable? One Nation's anti-Aboriginal policies and rhetoric helped define the party's position, but this was clearly not the only reason why electors voted for it in the Queensland state poll of 1998 or the October 1998 federal election. The disturbing thing is that the promise to expropriate all Aboriginal native title rights was not a sufficiently extreme policy to dissuade large numbers of people from voting for the party – over one million in the federal campaign.

The federal government, One Nation, state premiers, mining and farming lobbyists all had in common the objective of using legislation to reduce the already limited Aboriginal rights over pastoral lease land recognised by the High Court in Wik. The view seemed to be that the Court had suddenly produced rights that had never existed before and which could just as quickly be dispatched. There appeared to be little sense of the gravity of what was being proposed – the final extinguishment of rights which had come down to the present along a chain of inheritance stretching back into the far distant past which had survived the killing times, the demographic catastrophe which accompanied settlement, and the general disruption of the post-contact era. The fact that they were rights which had been recognised by the imperial government in the middle of the nineteenth century appeared to be little understood. But the message was there for all who chose to see. The aristocratic gentlemen who ran the Colonial Office in the 1840s were willing to concede more to indigenous Australians than the leaders of modern Australia, who professed to govern in the interests of all and to observe internationally recognised human rights. There was also little awareness in the policies and rhetoric of conservative political figures of the critical importance of access to land for the health and even the survival of traditional cultures. The fact that extinguishment of property rights and the closing-off of access to traditional lands might have serious consequences for already threatened tribal traditions never seemed to elicit sympathy or concern.

The long and intense debate over the Wik case and the government's legislative response to it both suggested that Aboriginal property rights were not considered to be as sacrosanct as those of other groups. It would clearly have been unthinkable for an Australian government to have advocated the expropriation of the property rights of any other distinguishable minority in Australian society. Any public figure who suggested that Chinese Australians or Hungarian Australians or Jewish Australians, for instance, should have their property expropriated would be reviled and shunned. Why is it possible to talk openly about bucket-loads of extinguishment when it is Aboriginal property that is in question?

The answer clearly lies deep in Australia's historical experience. To say that it is a manifestation of racism takes us some distance towards an explanation but not far enough. It is obvious that the doctrine of terra nullius still holds sway. It may have been expelled from the courts but it still resides securely in many hearts and minds. As a nation we find it very hard to recognise our own distinctive forms of racism. They are almost too close to us to be noticed. They exist in heavily disguised form, having long ago taken on local colour and become entwined in habit and custom and ways of thinking which are often taken as no more than common sense. This must surely be the explanation for the view frequently articulated by conservative intellectuals and commentators that there was no overt racism in the policies of One Nation or in the rhetoric of the NP and the NFF. It also helps us to understand the behaviour of Tim Fischer, who strongly condemned One Nation's policies towards Asian migration while joining them in calls for extinguishment. In his eyes, discrimination towards Asians was unacceptable but expropriation from Aborigines could be enthusiastically endorsed.

At the very time that Tim Fischer and other leaders of his party were attacking the Wik decision, he co-sponsored with the Minister for Foreign Affairs, Alexander Downer, a White Paper on Australia's foreign and trade policies entitled *In the National Interest*. The Ministers discussed the principles which underpinned Australia's outlook on the world and declared that they had a deep commitment to human rights. The government, they explained:

> views human rights as an inseparable part of Australia's overall foreign policy approach, both because the treatment of human beings is a matter of concern to Australians and because promoting and protecting human rights underpins Australia's broad security and economic interests.

Government policy, the Ministers declared, was based on the 'universality of fundamental human rights – civil, political, economic, social and cultural'.

Central to the values of the government was an 'unqualified commitment to racial equality and to eliminating racial discrimination'. This was, indeed, a 'non-negotiable tenet' of Australian policy making because the rejection of racial discrimination was not only a moral issue, it was also fundamental to our acceptance by, and engagement with, the region. Racial discrimination, the White Paper announced in ringing prose, was 'not only morally repugnant, it repudiates Australia's best interests'.

Aboriginal leaders who were trying to defend their ancient property rights against frontal assault from the NP and the NFF could be excused for wondering whether the Tim Fischer of the White Paper was the same one whom they knew to be barnstorming the country calling for bucket-loads of extinguishment. Was this simply a case of audacious hypocrisy, or was there a deeper problem at work? Did the Minister think that indigenous property rights were not really human rights at all? Or did indigenous Australians not qualify for them?

The hostile reaction to the Wik decision shows us just how difficult it is to redress historic injustice. The process of change has to push against the grain, against inherited habits of thought and feeling. Underlying much of the opposition to the recognition of Aboriginal property rights there appeared to be a powerful, if rarely expressed, feeling that the Aborigines didn't deserve such recognition. 'Why them?', people seemed to be saying. It was bad enough to recognise land rights; it added insult to injury to afford to those rights all the protection of private property inbuilt over the centuries into the common law. And it wasn't just the land itself, but the fact that land afforded status, as it has always done, and that the change of status brought about by Mabo and Wik threatened long accustomed patterns of hierarchy and subordination.

The question of native title and pastoral leases in Western Australia and the Northern Territory was contested again late in 1998, in the case of *Ward v. Western Australia* in the Federal Court. The two governments in question argued that the grant of a pastoral lease extinguished native title, a proposition comprehensively rejected by Mr Justice Lee, who strongly affirmed the principle of coexistence of lessees and native title holders. Lee recognised that native title was a prior interest in the land predating the pastoral lease, which had in fact been 'moulded to coexist with the exercise of the existing rights of Aboriginal people'.

But the judge was called on to do more than determine the question of extinguishment. He was obliged to assess what rights native title holders possessed, and the list was considerably more extensive than most observers had imagined. They could:

- possess, occupy, use, enjoy and have access to the land in question
- control the access of others to the land
- use and enjoy the resources
- control the use and enjoyment of others on those resources
- receive a portion of any resources taken by others
- maintain and protect places of importance under traditional laws, customs and practices
- maintain, protect and prevent the misuse of cultural knowledge of the native title holders.

It is an important and impressive portfolio of rights which gives real substance to Aboriginal rights on pastoral lease land.

An old and unique form of tenure, distinctively Australian, that has been in place for almost three-quarters of the time that Europeans have lived on the continent has suddenly and dramatically assumed immense contemporary importance. Mr Justice Lee's decision in *Ward v. Western Australia* was brought down almost exactly 150 years after Earl Grey declared that the British government neither would nor could exclude the Aborigines from access to, or the use 'they had been accustomed to make of', the vast pastoral lands of Australia. The pastoral lease was the one enduring and effective monument to British humanitarian aspirations – the one attempt to accord justice which worked, even though it has taken a century and a half for the full legal implications of the pastoral lease to unfold. Grey's insistence that Aborigines and pastoralists had mutual, albeit different, rights to the same land is reverberating throughout rural Australia. He believed that in taking control of the land the colonists entered into obligations 'of the most sacred kind' and were required to adequately compensate the traditional landowners. That historic promise of compensation, of an 'equivalence', will now perhaps finally be fulfilled.

Despite this weight of history and the accompanying power of legal precedent which judges have found persuasive in the Mabo, Wik and Ward cases, the decisions have been attacked as examples of the way in which fashionable feelings of guilt have led the judiciary astray, persuading it to collectively don the black armband of revisionist history.

XV

Paying Tribute to the Black Pioneers

During the lead-up to the Bicentenary celebrations of 1988 many Australians discussed their history and reflected on the progress of the previous 200 years. There was much talk about the pioneers and their achievements, great satisfaction about the legacy they had left behind them. In many letters to the papers and in comments contributed to talkback radio programs, white Australians not only celebrated the story of colonisation. They also compared the achievements with what they liked to term the primitive stagnation of Aboriginal society, which had never been able to emerge from the Stone Age. They argued that the success of nation-building was, in itself, justification for the original annexation and subsequent dispossesion of the indigenous tribes who had been unable to develop the land. The Aborigines, it was frequently asserted, played no part in the great saga of settlement. Pioneering was pre-eminently the work of the white settlers. It was they who founded the great rural industries, tamed the land and made it productive.

These are deeply held views. I used to hear them from students. Again and again they would say that the Aborigines did not deserve any special consideration because 'we had pioneered the land'. Having thought about the best way of answering this claim, I asked my students to help me conduct an imaginary exercise in family history. I suggested that in our survey we choose a random ten white and ten black Australians from anywhere but the most remote areas and that we investigate whether their families had a tradition of pioneering. Many of the ten white families would be quickly disqualified because they had arrived in Australia in the great wave of postwar migration or because their forebears had disembarked in the port cities and stayed there. Few families would have an authentic claim to a pioneering heritage. The opposite, I argued, would almost certainly be true in respect of the imaginary sample of Aboriginal families. All would have been involved in pioneering themselves or had parents or grandparents who had been, who had worked for most of their life as stockworkers, shepherds, drovers, divers or housemaids in remote areas of the continent.

One of the most common facts about the old people that Mabo, Loos and I met and interviewed in Townsville in the mid-1970s was that they had spent their lifetime in hard, demanding and often dangerous work. Their bodies bore the imprint of that work – their necks and arms were often ravaged by the sun, bodies stooped, hands roughly callused. Some of the old Islanders were in poor health as a consequence of diving too often and too deeply. They had suffered collapsed lungs and burst eardrums. Old stockmen talked lightly of broken arms, legs and ribs, which had often been crudely set without medical assistance. An old woman had lost her hand and lower arm many years before when she worked with a white tin miner on a small claim and had been blown up by an incompetently set charge of dynamite. Such men and women had frequently been taken by the white people to work when they were children and had laboured all their lives, often from dawn to dusk with few holidays. The meagre pay was normally placed in savings accounts for them, to be supervised by the local Protector of Aborigines who could decide whether or not any money could be drawn out. Money often disappeared from the accounts. But despite the hardships, the old people were almost universally proud of their achievements, of their skills and endurance. They took pleasure from the fact that they had worked so hard in their lifetime. They had a sense of achievement.

One of our interviewees subsequently wrote a letter to the local paper about his working life:

When I was eight years old, I worked on stations from 1923–1929 for nothing, and there were no schools for me, my brothers and sisters. In 1926, I was taken out of the mustering camp by my boss, who thought I was getting too heavy for the horses, and put into another job as dam sinker. I worked behind a scoop with three horses. I was 14 years old. My wage was 10 shillings a week, plus keep. My keep consisted of a swag on the ground in the bush, corned beef, tea, damper and treacle . . .

Women and children back at the station were fed like animals. Food was placed in a bowl and all had to eat out of the same bowl with a spoon or their hands . . .

In 1919, I remember the times when the young, a few men and teenage boys were called by the boss to get up at daylight for work – if they didn't get up immediately, the boss would belt them with a greenhide rope. Our day's work began at sunrise and finished at sunset, six days a week with Sundays off, but in the mustering camps work was every day until finished.

Over a great number of years in North Queensland I met many elderly Aborigines, over and above those we had interviewed. They had similar stories to tell of their life of arduous labour in all the major rural industries – mining, farming, grazing and pearling. After only a limited amount of research I came to realise that such men and women could be found in every town and community in north and central Australia. These were the people who, according to populist rhetoric, played no significant part in the settlement of the land. Indigenous people have suffered many injustices at the hands of white Australia. This lack of recognition, this profound disavowal, must be one of the most hurtful. The sad fact is that indigenous people themselves are often not fully aware of the contribution made all over Australia by Aboriginal and Torres Strait Islander guides, troopers, trackers, stockmen and -women, seamen and divers to the development of the country. They know their own stories and those of their friends and relatives, but there has never been any widespread public recognition, or celebration, of the black pioneers to which they could relate.

Like practically all Australians of my generation I found that at school, national history was overwhelmingly about explorers. We read or were told of the crossing of the Blue Mountains; we heard of the noble Sturt and his voyage along the Murray, of Eyre's epic journey across the Nullarbor and of the tragic fate of

Burke and Wills. We wrote projects and drew pictures and charts. On national maps we marked the assorted expeditions as they uncovered the mysteries of the inland. In the back of my primary-school atlas was a series of maps illustrating the progress of exploration. In the beginning the map of the continent was black apart from a pinpoint of yellow representing the settlement of Sydney Cove. As the expeditions ventured forth by land and sea, the area of yellow grew and the black contracted away into the most remote corners of the continent.

By these means we learnt that the explorers were the heroes of our history. The achievements of each expedition were always seen as those of the leader. I'm not sure we even knew how many other people accompanied Sturt or Mitchell or Oxley. We were told of the faithful 'black boys' who travelled with Eyre and who tried to save the hapless Kennedy in the jungles of Cape York, but we had no idea that Aborigines were the advisers, the consultants, whose skill and knowledge made all the difference between success and failure.

Coming back to the history of exploration many years later and reading systematically through all the published accounts of expeditions, I saw the whole scene with new eyes. I quickly appreciated that the often nameless 'black boys' played a critical role in almost every expedition and that this had been so from the very beginning. The value of Aboriginal assistance was recognised within the first few years of settlement. In 1791 Captain Watkin Tench led one of the first expeditions inland from Sydney. He was accompanied by two Aborigines, Colbee and Bolanderie, whom he hoped would supply the Europeans with 'much information relating to the country' and to their 'manner of living in the woods and the resources they rely upon in their journeys'. They quickly displayed their ease in the bush. 'The hindrances to walking . . . which plagued and entangled us so much', Tench wrote, 'seemed not to be heeded by them, and they wound through them with ease'.

Maritime expeditions also included Aboriginal guides. During his voyage of circumnavigation in 1802, Matthew Flinders was assisted by the Sydney Aboriginal identity Bongaree, who invariably led landing parties ashore and frequently brought about 'a friendly intercourse with the inhabitants of other parts of the coast'.

Expeditions moving inland would normally recruit Aboriginal guides from the stations they passed through on their way into the unknown interior. They would characteristically wait until suitable guides had been recruited before moving on. Even when outside their own country the guides proved adept at navigation, at finding the easy gradients, the short cuts, the fords over waterways. Critically important was their capacity to track horses, bullocks or camels, which frequently strayed away from overnight camps. They could also quickly make bark shelters and bark canoes to transport stores over rivers and creeks. They could also find water and food where no white man was able to. Equally important were their knowledge of Aboriginal protocol and their diplomatic skills, which frequently provided for unmolested transit through tribal homelands.

The major Australian explorers – Sturt, Eyre, Mitchell, Leichhardt – were all highly appreciative of the contribution made by Aboriginal expertise to their successful expeditions. Eyre wrote that he had:

> always made it a point, if possible, to be accompanied by one or more natives, and I have often found great advantage from it.

Attached to an exploring party they are frequently invaluable, as their perceptive powers are very great, and enable them both to see and hear anything at a much greater distance than a European. In tracking stray animals, and keeping on indistinct paths, they display a degree of perseverance and skill that is really wonderful.

Thomas Mitchell made many references to his various guides in his journals. Writing of those who had accompanied him into modern-day Victoria, and especially the man known to the Europeans as Piper, he observed that:

in most of our difficulties by flood and field, the intelligence and skill of our sable friends made the 'white-fellows' appear rather stupid. They could read traces on the earth, climb trees, or dive into the water, better than the ablest of us. In tracing lost cattle, speaking to 'the wild natives', hunting, or diving, Piper was the most accomplished man in camp.

Piper's role in actually choosing the route for the party to take was apparent in Mitchell's journal. He wrote at one point:

The whole management of the chase now devolved on him [Piper] and the two boys . . . and the native party usually explored the woods with our dogs, for several miles in front of our column. The females kept nearer the party, and often gave us notice of obstacles, in time to enable me to avoid them. My question on occasions was . . . Which way shall we go? to which one of the party would reply, pointing in the proper direction.

Having researched and written articles about the role of Aborigines in the achievements of the large official exploring expeditions, I turned my attention to the small private parties which followed the explorers' tracks into the inland. In dozens of diaries, letters and books the men and women pioneers paid tribute to their Aboriginal assistants. A visitor to New South Wales in the 1820s observed that when a colonist went into the bush he was generally accompanied by a 'party of blacks as porters of his luggage and conductors of his route'. In early Victoria black guides were 'found of infinite service to travellers' as a result of their 'knowledge of locality, quickness of perception, endurance of fatigue, their facility in procuring water and sustenance'. Rachel Henning, who settled with her brother in central Queensland in the 1860s, noted that people who were going on a long journey always took black guides with them because they were 'most useful servants in the bush'.

But they were much more than servants. They were teachers and instructors, educating Europeans both about the country itself and about the bushcraft which had evolved to make it possible to live comfortably within it. That is where the legendary Australian bushman learnt his skills. The well-known nineteenth-century bushman John F. Mann explained that as a young man he felt he needed to secure 'some knowledge of bush lore' before going up country. He was fortunate in falling in with 'a most intelligent Aborigine' who gave him 'much valuable information'. Many other pioneer settlers paid tribute to what they had learnt from their Aboriginal guides and advisers. A settler in early Victoria explained that the blacks not only 'guided us accurately, but taught us many lessons in bushcraft'.

One obvious conclusion I was able to draw from reading

innumerable accounts of frontier conflict was that the settlers were unable to match Aboriginal bushcraft. This was particularly true of the early years of colonisation. Attempts by soldiers or parties of vengeful settlers to come up with them usually ended in failure. Edward Eyre understood that in the bush the Aborigines had the advantage over the Europeans 'that a swimmer has in the water over the man who cannot swim'. In Tasmania, settlers despaired of ever being able to catch the marauding war parties. A retired army captain told the government that the blacks were seldom pursued, 'from a despair of finding them in the almost inaccessible fastnesses'. A colleague observed: 'I assure you they are a most intricate set of people to capture. No-one can conjecture how crafty and subtle they act in the bush'. The obvious answer to the settlers' difficulties was to recruit Aborigines to assist in pursuit and capture. In Tasmania, mainland Aborigines were hired by John Batman to pursue the Islanders. But the idea was institutionalised in Port Phillip in 1842 with the establishment of the first native police force. A second force was sent to the northern frontiers of New South Wales in 1848. It was taken over by the new Queensland government in 1859 and continued to ride around the fringes of European settlement until the end of the century.

The squatter-dominated Queensland government enthusiastically supported the force, which was used to crush Aboriginal resistance and thereby facilitate the rapid occupation of the colony's vast pastoral lands. The white officers were instructed to 'disperse any large assemblage of blacks' at all times and opportunities. The force was brutally effective, combining European weapons and horses and Aboriginal bushcraft. It was also cheap, the troopers receiving only a fraction of the money which would have been required to attract white recruits. Almost no infrastructure was required. While out in the field the troopers hunted and foraged for food and they were provided with living quarters which no white man would accept. A further advantage was that the troopers could engage in acts which were illegal and could not be questioned in a court because their evidence was not admissible.

The Queensland Native Police had an evil reputation in the colonies. The force was frequently attacked by humanitarian reformers, and scandals constantly erupted over brutal dispersals. The various administrations persisted with it because it was seen to be so effective in achieving the military defeat of tribes throughout the colony. In the other colonies the police forces employed large numbers of 'black trackers', who provided the bush skills necessary to counter the clans resisting European incursions. This was particularly so in areas of rugged terrain like the Kimberleys. As well as the troopers and trackers formally employed by colonial police forces, there were countless 'tame blacks' who accompanied and assisted the private punitive expeditions which rode out to attack local Aborigines in every part of the country. Almost every Aborigine I talked to over the years knew stories about the destructiveness and violence of the Native Police. In some communities the memories of massacre were vividly alive. The horror of it all could still be recalled. Few of my informants were able to distinguish between the normal colonial/state police force and the parliamentary Native Police. So the contemporary police force often had to cope with ancestral memories of indiscriminate killing, abduction and rape. In recent years the police had been quite consciously trying to live that reputation down.

Even a brief acquaintance with elderly Aboriginal men and

women provides an insight into their importance in the pastoral industry and of the significance of stockwork in their lives. The historical record showed how deeply rooted the link was in Australia's past. There was an obvious and common transition from guide and adviser to professional pastoral worker. Most parties who went out 'looking for country' took Aboriginal guides who were already working on established sheep and cattle stations. The official Protector of Aborigines in Victoria in the 1840s, G.A. Robinson, observed that it was the Aborigines who:

> first guided White Man through the intricacies of their forests, led them to their Rivers, their springs, and rich pastures, and assisted them in keeping their stock, watching their working oxen, tracking their stray horses, and rendering other essential assistance.

Aborigines accompanied the squatters into new country, and in north Australia they became the mainstay of the industry. There was never enough white labour in the more remote parts of the continent. White stockmen were expensive to employ and were notoriously unreliable, coming and going at will. At the end of the nineteenth century black workers outnumbered white by five or six to one in many parts of the north. Most Aborigines worked on their own country. They had strong motivation to stay where they were and in fact had never conceded ownership to the white boss, who nevertheless had to be managed, appeased and kept satisfied. Without Aboriginal workers most outback stations would have collapsed into bankruptcy within a matter of months. The labour was cheap to employ – usually acquired by payment of tobacco, clothing, tea and sugar. It was the low cost of labour which made many stations viable. That was how they remained competitive. Large areas of cheap land were not enough. Without Aboriginal stockmen and -women the land had no value.

A historian of Aboriginal labour in the Queensland pastoral industry, Dawn May, estimated that at the turn of the century at least four blacks could be employed for the cost of one white stockman who earned about £100 a year. A government official in Western Australia who investigated the situation of Aboriginal labour on outback sheep stations in 1882 reported that:

> the settlers take a business view of the position; they argue that unless the natives can be utilized as shepherds, sheep farming on the Gascoyne will not pay. A white man costs £50 per annum and his food, and it requires a cart, or at least a pack horse, to move him from one part of the run to another, a native will do the same work for his food, and a shirt occasionally, and he requires no assistance in moving with his sheep from one camp to another.

Twenty years later another official found Aboriginal labour even more important for the ninety or so sheep stations between the DeGray and Ashburton rivers. On average there were twenty-five workers per station, but some were home to sixty or seventy. Practically all the work was done by the Aborigines. As well as shepherding they did the housework, cooking, shearing, wool scouring, carting, blacksmithing, pitsawing and fencing.

Pastoralists did not provide any housing. Their workers lived in the 'blacks' camp', situated far enough away from the homestead to be out of earshot but close enough to call up workers for the house and garden when they were required. At times when demand for workers was high – at mustering or shearing – more camp-dwellers could be drawn into the workforce and then sent back to the camp when not required. The same pattern was apparent across the working year. In the dry season many of the men and some of the women were needed to muster, cull, brand and fence. When the wet arrived the whole camp would 'go bush' and return to traditional life for a few months.

Black labour was skilled as well as cheap. Aborigines brought into the station economy all the intimate knowledge of the country – its topography and botany, the swing of the seasons, the sources of water and grass. They could track sheep and cattle with an ease which few white station workers ever managed to rival. They quickly learnt how to ride, break and manage horses and how to work with sheep and cattle. The older men took on the responsibility of teaching the young ones all they needed to know to become valuable stockworkers. It was the distinctive skills of Aboriginal workers which made it possible to run sheep, and above all cattle, profitably on large, unfenced and unimproved stations. In his reminiscences of pastoral life in central Queensland, A.C. Grant observed:

> Day by day the cattle on the camps were gone through and absent ones noted and searched for until found. In this duty the black boys were simply invaluable and their interest in the work and untiring skill in tracking contributed chiefly to the success which attended the pioneers in keeping their herds together.

A pioneer of stations around the Gulf of Carpentaria came to the point more quickly in 1884, observing that 'I don't know what we pioneers should have done without the blacks, for they can't be beat at looking after horses and cattle'.

Aboriginal women, or the 'house gins' as they were called, carried out much of the domestic labour on the sheep and cattle stations right across north Australia. They drew water from wells or nearby rivers for the garden and the household. They washed and scrubbed and ironed, cooked and gardened. Many white children were cared for by Aboriginal nursemaids. Like male workers, the women were unpaid even though they often worked very long hours. A Queensland government official who visited a large number of stations in the south-west of the colony in 1900 found only two cases where the women were paid anything at all, even though the station owners admitted that their black servants did work for which they would have to pay a white woman fifteen shillings or one pound a week.

Enough has been said to show how grossly unfair it is to say that Aborigines and Torres Strait Islanders had no part in the pioneering and development of Australia, that the European settlers did it all themselves. This is especially so in the north and centre of the continent, where indigenous men and women made up the bulk of the workforce and where Asian and Melanesian migrants also made a significant contribution. Indigenous labour was widely employed in all the major towns scattered across the north. A pioneer resident of Gladstone observed that the 'town blacks' were 'an almost necessary social auxiliary – ministering to our wants and necessities in fifty different ways'. A young woman who went to live in Normanton in 1895 found she had 'nothing to do' but practise her music because 'we have black labour for all jobs'.

All around the north coast, from Broome in the west to

Mackay in the east, Aborigines and Torres Strait Islanders worked in the sea-based industries of pearling and bêche-de-mer collecting and processing. Their labour was critically important in the early history of pearling during the period when shells were collected by skindiving in shallow water. On the Western Australian coast 400 to 500 Aborigines were employed on the luggers. In 1869 a lugger master explained how he prepared for a new season on the pearling beds: 'you take the first of the ebb and glide away out of the creek . . . then comes the most important part . . . the picking up of niggers . . . for pearling after all would never pay white labour'. Aborigines were often forced to work on the luggers, were marooned on offshore islands in the lay-off, were unpaid, poorly fed and chronically overworked.

The size of the indigenous labour force in north Australia may surprise many people brought up on stories of enterprising white pioneers. The labour was very cheap, and the workers could be coerced with fist, boot, stockwhip and revolver without fear of social opprobrium or legal action. The gap between the productivity of black labour and the return to the indigenous worker was striking. In modern-day terms, indigenous labour must have contributed tens of millions of dollars to white bosses and to the settler economy as a whole. One day someone should attempt to estimate just how much that figure might have been.

It was the pastoral industry that always absorbed the largest amount of black labour and saw the emergence of a system which combined aspects of a western market and a traditional economy. The industry ruthlessly exploited Aboriginal workers, but they were able to remain on their own land and to keep their communities together. Stockwork was incorporated into modified forms of traditional culture and provided meaningful work and a subordinate but recognised role in the European economy. Aborigines took pride in their mastery of all the skills required of the competent stockworker.

After spending many years researching the early history of the pastoral industry and supervising the related work of several of my postgraduate students, I was convinced that the industry owed a profound debt to Aboriginal Australia which has never been acquitted. Many modern graziers either don't know or deny this history. I can remember the deep sense of injustice I felt when I first visited the Stockman's Hall of Fame at Longreach, which for a long time scarcely mentioned Aborigines. Even now there is no real indication there of the critical role played by black labour in the foundation and survival of the industry. It was at the Hall of Fame that graziers from many parts of Australia gathered in 1997 to demand that the Prime Minister legislate to extinguish all Aboriginal rights over land held under pastoral leases. The cultural links between indigenous people and land had survived all the traumas of colonisation – but what the graziers were asking would sever these links with just one new law.

XVI

Writing Black-armband History

The historians of the black-armband brigade who have rewritten the story of the relations between Aborigines and settlers during the last thirty years have been accused of many things. Critics complain that they wallow in guilt and steep their history in their own paranoia, that they illegitimately impose contemporary standards on the past, and that their objectivity is compromised by too rigid an adherence to political correctness. The more vociferous opponents of revisionist history go much further and accuse the practitioners of deliberately undermining national cohesion and self-confidence and making the young feel ashamed rather than proud of their past.

I am unable to speak for my colleagues, but little of the criticism appears to have much to do with what I think I have been doing since 1970 and why I have done it. I have been aware of the attacks – both personal and general – but they usually seem to be off target, to have missed the point. I don't think I have ever felt guilty about historic events, regardless of how infamous. I have always thought that guilt pertained to those things – actions, words, thought even – for which one is personally responsible. I am not sure that I have ever felt shame about the brutal business of colonisation, perhaps because I don't have a strong enough sense of identification with the British colonists who thrust the frontiers out into Aboriginal Australia. I have often been incensed or angry about the cruelty and injustice involved, but even then I have felt under a professional obligation to try to understand and explain the behaviour of the perpetrators. To know *why* was more important and more challenging than simply to descry. I have long believed that evasion and hypocrisy should be exposed and that the truth about the past must be laid out and subjected to scrutiny. The colonists were prone to hypocrisy, were unwilling to grasp the reality of dispossession, and talked of empty lands awaiting their first owner and of indigenous people melting away in some inexplicable manner.

I thought from the beginning of my career that historical writing was inescapably political – the history of race relations especially so. How could I pretend otherwise? Historians do not shed their ideological clothing or their personal feelings when they venture back into the past seeking to hear the words and to enter the minds and hearts of their chosen subjects. The historian cannot be sundered from the citizen. Present values and preoccupations will always help to determine which aspects of the past will be thought important, which questions pursued, examined and exhibited. But most of the issues which have disturbed the critics of black-armband history were not carried from present to past in historians' briefcases; they were there waiting for them on the ground, unmistakable and unavoidable. Many of the revisionist historians would share a broad political agenda and common sympathies, but their ideas would not distinguish them from great numbers of people in the general population. There is no exclusive, self-selected caste of black-armband scholars. Sometimes they display a zealous denial of any taint of racism, a prejudice in favour of the Aborigines and Islanders. But even then few historians would see themselves as being governed by political correctness, or not as that term is commonly understood. They do not feel the need to be correct themselves as much as desiring to correct the history distorted by several generations of nationalist and self-congratulatory writing, which had banished the Aborigines from text to melancholy footnote and thereby expurgated most of the violence and much of the injustice.

I am not aware of any historian who has consciously set out to undermine social cohesion, damage the nation or corrupt youth. I doubt that any think they could even if they wanted to. Much critical, revisionist history springs from a belief that Australia should do better and is capable of doing so. It is written in hope and expectation of reform, crafted in the confidence that carefully marshalled, clearly expressed argument can persuade significant numbers of Australians to change their minds and redirect their sympathies. Beyond that confidence in individuals is a firm belief in the capacity of Australian democracy to respond to new ideas which in time can reshape policies and recast institutions, laws and customs. Many historians have worked with the same confidence that inspired Mabo – and for that matter the elders of the Wik, Thayorre, Miruiwung and Gajirong peoples – that Australian society is committed to fairness, that it can be persuaded to take the high road away from injustice despite long residence among it.

Most of those who wrote and spoke and acted to bring about change sought not to undermine but to strengthen Australian democracy, by dealing with its most obvious deficiency, to bring to fruition the long-delayed promise to treat all people equally regardless of racial origin. At the moment of its flowering in the late nineteenth century and early twentieth century, Australian liberalism was blighted by racism. All the fine words and noble sentiments about democracy and liberty and a fair go for all only applied to white men and subsequently and often grudgingly to white women. There was a problem, too, in the heart of liberalism itself. Its most notable and influential apostle, John Stuart Mill, wrote of the need for the individual to have liberty from the power of the state and the conformist embrace of community, but he also spoke of the right of the nation to foster its own internal cohesion and cast out or deny membership to those who were different in culture or traditions.

There was another way in which the revisers and the reinterpreters showed their respect for the Australia they addressed and whose interest and concern they courted. They acted on the assumption that a nation did not need to get its history wrong, as a French nineteenth-century intellectual once famously suggested. They believed that it was time for Australia to come face to face with its past, to cast off the evasion and avoidance, that contemporary society could cope with the truth and find it bracing and challenging rather than threatening. It was time, too, to throw back the veil which early generations had drawn over the brutal history of the frontier. Australians no longer needed to cling to those comforting legends of the empty land, peaceful settlement, the heroic and bloodless conquest of the inland, the unarmed frontiersmen singing to the cattle.

While drawing attention to the high human cost of colonisation, I never felt that it cancelled out or made void all the many achievements of the settlers and their Australian-born descendants – founding the great primary industries, creating institutions and infrastructure, building towns and cities, and nurturing one of the world's most impressive democracies. While I wrote on and researched in the history of indigenous–settler relations, I taught comprehensive courses about Australian history and politics for many years and in the process paid tribute to the many and varied achievements of the two centuries of European occupation. When in Sydney in January 1988 I attended both great commemorations – the arrival of the tall ships in the morning and the Aboriginal march and rally in the afternoon. I was surprised when several earnest young people chided me for wanting to be there when the arrival of the First Fleet was commemorated.

In writing extensively about dispossession I haven't myself felt dispossessed. I am unable to share the view of those who feel they don't really belong in Australia, that they are barely tolerated guests or that they will always be so alienated from the land that they can't even contemplate being buried in Australian soil. I don't relate to Australia as a whole: it is much too large and much too diverse. But I cannot remember a time when I didn't feel at home in Tasmania. It has little to do with the will or the intellect. You either feel you belong or you don't. And once that sense is there it can't be given up, willed away or reasoned out of existence. Almost thirty years of writing revisionist history changed my views about many things, but never touched my sense of where I had come from, where I belonged and where since early childhood I had known the wind, the sky and the silver slanting light.

Just as I was required to justify to my idealistic young critics why I was quite comfortable about watching the re-enactment of the arrival of the First Fleet, I often found myself defending Australia from extreme and sweeping attacks made both inside and outside the country. I did this partly from a spontaneous reaction to unreasoned zealotry and a rejection of the view that Australia is the most bigoted and racist society in the world. I have always opposed the habit of making things out to be worse than they actually are in the present or were in the past. Exaggeration is neither intellectually credible nor politically astute, and makes it impossible to distinguish between degrees of oppression or grades of intolerance. There is a linked tendency to argue that nothing has improved, a sort of public-spirited masochism, the devotees of which feel better the worse things can be made to appear.

Having lived in provincial north Australia for more than thirty years, I have never doubted that racism continues to be a powerful ever-present force. I was not at all surprised by the sudden emergence of the One Nation party or by the level of support it received. But what seems to be the most significant thing about contemporary Australia is not that racism is still endemic but that it is not more apparent than it is, given its importance in the past and the almost universal commitment to a white Australia right up to the 1960s. In the past thirty years the country has changed far more rapidly than might have been expected. I think the retreat from the racist heritage is far more noteworthy than its surviving manifestations. But this is a hard case to argue with young people, who often combine a laudable rejection of racism with a lack of sympathy for older Australians. My students often ask how it was that people in the past held such objectionable views, how they could be so terrible. They have no understanding of just how pervasive racial thought was a generation or two ago, how the Second World War and the Holocaust marked an intellectual watershed after which nothing would be the same again. And so they find it easy and natural to condemn those older Australians who cling to ideas taught to them in far-off days when they were young and which at the time were sanctioned by scholars, scientists and statesmen.

Experience outside Australia also helps to sharpen the perspective and season the judgement. It is obvious that indigenous and tribal peoples are badly treated in many parts of the world. That in itself should never be accepted as an excuse for what happens here. We must be judged by standards we espouse and commitments we mouth. But in many countries the leaders of minority groups are silenced, imprisoned, tortured, murdered – or just ignored. Indigenous Australians have achieved a prominence in public life, a moral and discursive authority scarcely matched anywhere. In a similar way indigenous culture – painting and design, literature, dance, drama – has a prominence almost unrivalled elsewhere. That is a tribute both to the leading figures of the Aboriginal renaissance and to Australian society as a whole, which both welcomed and nurtured the upsurge of creativity – although conscientious people continue to worry about where appreciation ends and appropriation begins.

Discussion overseas soon makes it clear how important for Australia the High Court's Mabo decision was. The word Mabo has become known all over the world as a symbol of the struggle of indigenous people for land and justice. I have heard the judgement praised by leading academics in Canada, by prominent Indian leaders in the United States, by Norway's Chief Justice, by the chairman of New Zealand's Waitangi Tribunal and by senior jurists in South Africa. In Adelaide I met by chance a delegation of young Masai men and women from Kenya who had come to Australia because they had heard of Mabo; they thought it would help them in the struggle to retain control of their traditional lands, which the government was granting to others on the assumption that a nomadic lifestyle did not establish true title to the soil. But assertion of terra nullius is not confined to Africa. The Swedish courts have also determined that the Sami people of the north have not acquired title to traditional territory because reindeer herders could not be considered to be in actual occupation of the land. Like the Masai, the Sami no doubt wish that the spirit of Mabo and Wik would blow through their own courts.

Other aspects of the situation in Australia attract admiration or concern overseas. Margaret and I had a formal meeting in Mexico with the recently appointed National Commission for Indigenous People. Some of the members seemed almost alarmed at what they perceived to be Australian radicalism. Leaders of the American Indian Law Alliance were greatly impressed by the funding for indigenous programs; an old Mapuche Indian elder in Chile had tears in his eyes when I assured him that the Australian government provided money to buy back Aboriginal land. Ainu leaders in Japan and Sami leaders in Norway and Sweden complained that there was little interest in their situation in their own countries and said that they envied Aborigines and Islanders. It is not unusual to find young Scandinavians, in Australia to study Aboriginal issues, who know almost nothing about the Sami.

While my overseas experience has provided valuable comparative insights, allowing me to see how outsiders view Australia, it has been my life in Townsville that has provided me with much of what I know about the recent history and politics of race. I have seen and heard white and black Australians relating on a daily basis for over thirty years, have witnessed incidents that were shocking or inspiring, frightening or amusing. In the process I have stored away the impressions of half a lifetime, which have constantly enlightened my historical research and which, above all, have maintained my interest in race relations and prevented me from ever effectively pursuing numerous competing research interests which beckoned for a season or two. But in all the years of research, writing and lecturing I never doubted the contemporary relevance of what I was doing or lacked a sense of the great responsibility which rests on the shoulders of those who interpret the nation's past.

Much has changed in the thirty-four years since I walked across the tarmac at Townsville airport into the close embrace of a humid tropical night. But many things remain the same, or nearly so. It is still possible to find small camps of Aboriginal men and women around the town in the parks, on the beaches, in the shade of the huge, spreading fig and banyan trees. They spend a few days at each site and then move on, living rough and drinking hard, arousing hostility from the wider community, which every now and then demands that local or state governments 'do something' to deal with the problem. Indigenous people are far more likely to be caught up in the justice system than their white counterparts. Aborigines and Islanders make up over 60 per cent of inmates in the local prison at Stuart Creek on the outskirts of town.

But the great majority of the indigenous families which settled in Townsville in the 1960s and 1970s have been successful in the difficult and linked tasks of living in a city and being surrounded by migloos who often make watchful, censorious neighbours. Many families are still poor and struggle to make ends meet, but others have established themselves securely in the community. The educational standards of the young people are far higher than those of their parents who grew up on remote settlements or cattle stations. They have had longer and better schooling. Hundreds of indigenous students from all over North Queensland have passed successfully through the university and what was the Townsville College of Advanced Education before amalgamation in 1983. Many local indigenous organisations – schools, medical and legal services, a media company and radio station, housing cooperatives, cultural societies – have sprung up in the last generation. Some have failed amid accusations of incompetence and mismanagement, but others have been highly successful and have provided invaluable experience in leadership and administration.

Young Aborigines and Islanders often say that nothing has changed over the last thirty years, that things are as bad as ever. But that undersells both the achievements of their own community and the policies pursued by local, state and national governments. Their impatience and frustration is in itself a sign of change. They are far less resigned and submissive than their parents' generation. They know no deference. They are self-confident, assured and politically aware, and won't be pushed around or patronised by anyone. I can remember political meetings I attended twenty-five years ago where not a single indigenous person could be persuaded to stand up and speak in public. Nowadays articulate and forceful orators abound. They know all the ways in which to command an audience. It is the tentative, anxious migloos who are now uncertain about speaking and afraid of giving offence.

In Townsville indigenous urbanisation has succeeded. Aborigines and Islanders have colonised the whitefella city. In doing so their identity has been strengthened rather than weakened. Close proximity with white Australians has enhanced their sense of difference. At the same time, Aboriginal nationalism has brought people together whose backgrounds are quite different. The Aboriginal flag and the national colours of red, yellow and black are worn on shirts and dresses, shoes, earrings, bracelets, necklaces. The Islander community continues to identify strongly with the Torres Strait home islands, but the local families have usually been very successful in Townsville. They still have only limited dealings with the Aborigines and are often subject to hostility and suspicion and feel themselves to be barely tolerated migrants.

The white population has come to accept the presence of self-conscious Aboriginal and Islander communities as a normal part of life in Townsville while at the same time becoming, if anything, less tolerant of the social dissidents who camp out around the town. There is a wide range of opinion about the unmistakable improvement in indigenous living standards, education and social status and in the accompanying boost to communal self-confidence. At one end of the spectrum are those who applaud the obvious achievement and take comfort from it as a positive indication about Australian society; at the other end are people who are hostile to and threatened by the same developments. 'Uppity niggers' are still profoundly unsettling to some people. The desecration of Eddie Mabo's grave on the night of its unveiling was a clear case of the anger provoked by indigenous advancement and high achievement.

The classic racism of the sort expressed by the old men and

women we met in the 1960s is far less common now. The language and terminology have changed, although there are apparently many people who still believe that indigenous people are biologically inferior, referring now to genetics rather than to anatomy. On the morning of the 1998 Queensland state election a correspondent wrote to the *Townsville Daily Bulletin* explaining that high Aboriginal mortality rates and low educational achievement were due to 'endless ingrained apathy' which 'undoubtedly raises the question of the genetic quality of indigenous intelligence – to which there can be only one answer'.

Political correctness – so denounced by conservative politicians and commentators – had some positive effects in the north. Disapproval of overt racism grew, while the reception of racist jokes and anecdotes in social gatherings became harder to predict. The sanctioning of racism, the attacks on political correctness by the One Nation party and in a covert way by the Liberal and National parties, gave many bigots hope that the good old days had returned. Margaret and I had always known that when political leaders appeared to sanction or even promote racism, a minority would believe they had received approval to take action. This was brought home to us quite literally at the height of John Howard's campaign for 'One Australia' in the late 1980s. One morning we found the side of our garage daubed in red paint with the slogans:

ONE OZ   ASIANS OUT   NO ABOS

Hostility to land rights and ameliorative social programs found concrete political expression for the first time in the 1993 federal election. A local government solicitor, John Robinson, ran as an independent for the Townsville seat of Herbert, on a platform that was overwhelmingly concerned with Aboriginal issues and had some side attention to Asian migration.

The candidate demanded a referendum on the question of land rights because Aboriginal affairs were 'completely out of control'. The time had come, he believed, to declare that enough was enough, to 'say no to the land rights and Aboriginal affairs fiasco', otherwise Australia would 'continue to slide backwards as a nation, and as a people'. Although having little money to spend on the campaign the candidate was very successful, winning almost 14 per cent of the vote in a field of nine, more than doubling the total of the National Party candidate and winning three times the vote going to the Australian Democrats. It was a foretaste of the emergence of One Nation three years later, indicating that a substantial minority of voters were willing to abandon their traditional party allegiances for a candidate who campaigned almost exclusively on Aboriginal issues and on land rights, which at the time had no direct relevance to the local electorate at all.

A land claim in 1998 over Magnetic Island, just off the coast, deeply divided the community. The local Wulgurukaba people lodged a claim to crown land on the island which was largely occupied by a national park. Their main concerns were to have their traditional ownership recognised and to be consulted about the management of the park. The chairwoman of the Magnetic Island Community and Commerce Association welcomed the claim, looking forward to a boost in tourism given the interest of overseas visitors in Aboriginal history and culture. But another resident told the *Townsville Bulletin* that the whole island was 'enraged' because the Aborigines were claiming the island, 'which already belong[ed] to all Australians'. The local Liberty Party federal member said that he hoped the claim would be withdrawn. It was in the interests of Aborigines to do so because it would 'produce more bitterness'.

While Townsville had difficulty with the new world created by the Mabo judgement, it was also haunted by the violence of the past and the vigilante action taken by white men during much of the town's 120-year history. Early one morning in November 1992, two Aboriginal brothers were seen attempting to break into a car across the road from a popular nightclub. The car belonged to the manager of the club. The club bouncers, other staff members and several airforce personnel attending the club chased the two into nearby Ross Creek, shouting threatening racist abuse. Several of the pursuers dived into the water and dragged one of the brothers out. He was bashed when he was brought ashore. The other brother evaded capture after a struggle in the water and disappeared into the darkness. His drowned body was found in the creek the following day.

A taxi driver who witnessed the events told the inquest that he thought that the scene had resembled the 'Ku Klux Klan chasing a black man'. The men behaved like 'a mob of mongrel dogs'. The same observation was made later by a boat owner who had been asleep on his yacht in the marina. An Aboriginal man who was also a witness to the chase said he had heard a white man say: 'Kill the black c—'. He had thought, 'Something's going on here, they're killing Murris.'

The police arrived while the search was proceeding. They stood by and did nothing, allowing the pursuit to continue. Under examination at the inquest the local inspector agreed that the men were vigilantes and that he didn't approve of what had been done. But he didn't know what his officers could have done in the circumstances and he didn't think they should be criticised for their inaction.

The coroner decided that the young man had died by misadventure and no charges were to be laid. When questioned, the vigilantes said they felt they had a right to take the law into their own hands. The inspector and the coroner appeared to agree with them. It was, after all, an old, time-honoured custom in North Queensland. There appeared to be little public concern about the death of the young man. Clearly things would not have worked out the way they did if the roles had been reversed, if a twenty-two-year-old white man had drowned after diving into the creek while being pursued by an angry and vengeful group of Aborigines shouting racial abuse.

This discussion began with the observation that many Australians felt that they had been poorly served by their teachers and by the nation's historians. They are angry that they weren't told the truth about the past and feel they were denied information, interpretation and understanding. It is now possible to explore the past by means of large numbers of books, articles, films, novels, songs and paintings. Many voices have filled out the space once claimed by Stanner's Great Australian Silence. We can know a great deal about the history of indigenous–settler relations. But knowing brings burdens which can be shirked by those living in ignorance. With knowledge the question is no longer what we know but what we are now to do, and that is a much harder matter to deal with. It will continue to perplex us for many years to come.

Many things have changed since 1965. Much has been achieved. Tolerance and understanding have broadened out.

Bigotry is in retreat. But the racist past still weighs heavily on the present and might yet destroy any hope of reconciliation in this generation. Black-armband history is often distressing, but it does enable us to know and understand the incubus which burdens us all.

Index

ALSO BY
HENRY REYNOLDS

THE OTHER SIDE OF THE FRONTIER
Aboriginal Resistance to the European Invasion of Australia

Winner of the Ernest Scott Prize

Using documentary and oral evidence, much of it previously unpublished, Henry Reynolds sets out the Aboriginal reactions to the coming of the Europeans to Australia. Contrary to conventional beliefs the Aborigines were not passive: they resorted to guerilla warfare, sorcery, theft of white settlers' goods, crops and animals, retribution and revenge sallies, and the adaptation of certain of the newcomers' ways. In presenting this material, Reynolds challenges us to reconsider not only our interpretation of our history, but also the implications for future relations between the peoples of Australia.

'Reynolds has painted an exciting and compelling picture of . . . resistance seen from the Aboriginal side . . . In most cases Aborigines fought heroically against overwhelming odds and superior weapons to resist usurpation of their lands, their rights and their livelihood.'

Age Monthly Review

'This is the most important book ever on Aboriginal–European contact.'

National Times

Fate of a Free People

'I knew it was no use my people trying to kill all the white people
now, there were so many of them always coming in big boats.'

Truganini

In March 1847, Queen Victoria was presented with a petition for
justice signed by eight Tasmanian Aborigines living at Wybalenna
settlement on Flinders Island. This is the document at the heart
of Henry Reynolds' exciting reassessment of black/white conflict in colonial Tasmania.

Long misrepresented as an unequal struggle between civilisation
and childlike savages, the 'Black War' is shown to be much more
complex. The Aborigines defended their ancient homelands
with bushcraft and guerilla tactics, but realised there was only
one solution – a treaty guaranteeing peace in return for recom-
pense and a limited exile. Not prisoners on Flinders Island but
'a free people', the negotiators kept their promises though the
colonial government did not.

Even now the black and white fallen of Tasmania's patriotic
war are largely unacknowledged. Reynolds challenges us to face
our colonial history and accord this war the same honour as
Australia's conflicts overseas.

THE LAW OF THE LAND

'I am at a loss to conceive by what tenure we hold this country, for it does not appear to be that we either hold it by conquest or by right of purchase.'

G.A. Robinson, Tasmanian Protector of Aborigines, 1832

In this readable and dramatic book, Henry Reynolds reassesses the legal and political arguments used to justify the European settlement of Australia. His conclusions form a compelling case for the belief that the British government conceded land rights to the Aborigines early in the nineteenth century.

'Reynolds' is a project concerned with nothing less than the revision of our interpretations of ourselves as a people.'

Veronica Brady, *Australian Book Review*

'Propositions advanced in *The Law of the Land* overturn 200 years of white assumptions in Australia over who owns the land.'

Michael Davie, *London Observer*

'The duplicity of white Australia's reasoning is laid bare in a meticulous history with a strong moral purpose.'

Cassandra Pybus, *Top Shelf*

'This must be the most important book yet written concerning the Aborigines' basic rights to land.'

Bob Dixon, *Canberra Times*